Airliners of th

GERRY MANNING

Front cover image: So well-known was Concorde that people never said they had flown in 'a' Concorde, or even 'the Concorde'; it was, simply, Concorde. Pictured in July 1997 at RAF Fairford, Gloucestershire, is BAe/ Aérospatiale Concorde 102 G-BOAF c/n 216 of British Airways. This location was, in fact, where the prototypes had been tested. Its arrival was a supersonic charter flight, followed by a landing at the air show being held there. British Airways were the last to fly the Concorde, with services ending in October 2003. This aircraft was the last one ever to fly; it's final flight was on 26 November 2003, when it flew from London Heathrow to its birthplace of Filton to be preserved by the Bristol Aero Collection.

Back cover image: A view that cannot be repeated. It is August 1991, and a view from the control tower at Leningrad's Pulkovo Airport. All the aircraft belong to Aeroflot. A few days earlier the Moscow Coup had happened and failed, yet it was ultimately the event that led to the demise of the USSR. Soon, Leningrad would go back to being St Petersburg, the Aeroflot monopoly would be over, and this view would show a host of new airlines and colours schemes.

Acknowledgements
Thanks to Bob O'Brien for proofreading the captions.

Published by Key Books
An imprint of Key Publishing Ltd
PO Box 100
Stamford
Lincs PE19 1XQ

www.keypublishing.com

The right of Gerry Manning to be identified as the author of this book has been asserted in accordance with the Copyright, Designs and Patents Act 1988 Sections 77 and 78.

Copyright © Gerry Manning, 2021

ISBN 978 1 80282 023 2

Typeset by SJmagic DESIGN SERVICES, India.

Introduction

This is the fourth book in my series, Airliners of the Decade. The first, *Airliners of the 1960s* was published by Airlife in 2000; the second and third, *Airliners of the 1970s* and *Airliners of the 1980s* were published by Midland Publishing in 2005 and 2007, respectively. This latest work follows the same premise, to illustrate the range of both airliners and airlines that operated during the decade. It is, of course, impossible within the scope of a book of this size to cover all the carriers and types of aircraft to be seen during those years.

However, I have aimed to cover a wide selection of aircraft and airlines across a large geographical spread – from the small commuter aeroplanes to the large multi-engine, wide-bodied aircraft.

As through all decades, there were many important developments within the 1990s. One such development was the continuous rise of the Airbus consortium, which now had a full range of the most advanced aircraft on offer. They were able to take on and match the American manufacturers and outpace them in sales.

For the civil aircraft enthusiast, it was the political changes that made the biggest difference to their hobby. The civil war in Yugoslavia saw six new nations appear, but the biggest change was the demise of the Union of Soviet Socialist Republics (from here on referred to as the USSR) into 15 different independent republics. This led to new registration prefixes and the formation of many new airlines – in the case of the ex-USSR countries, the number ran into the hundreds. I could not resist the temptation to investigate the rise and fall of these new airlines and the aircrafts that they operated.

Within the captions, I have attempted to say who the airline was, or still is, the type of aircraft, and where and when the picture was taken. Lastly, I outline the fate of the illustrated aircraft. Since most aircraft are now leased rather than bought by airlines, there is a tendency to break up some airframes much earlier than would have happened in the past. This is because, in some cases, the aircraft is worth more for the sum value of all its spare parts than as a complete unit. When an aircraft moves to another airline, I have used the words 'sold on'; this covers both actual sales and it moving to a new lease.

At the time of writing, the COVID-19 pandemic is affecting the world's airlines. Many aircraft are in store in the short term, whilst other stored types may never resume service. It is difficult to be sure of the long-term consequences of the slow return to the kind of operations that took place pre-pandemic.

All pictures are from my own travels and scanned from Fujichrome slides.

Gerry Manning, Liverpool
May 2021

Airliners of the 1990s

The Boeing 707 was not the first jet airliner to fly, nor was it the first to enter service or the first to operate across the Atlantic Ocean. However, it was, without a doubt, the most successful of all the early jet-powered airliners. Its first commercial service was with the launch customer Pan American (PanAm), on 26 October 1958, with a flight from New York to Paris, France. By the 1990s, most 707s left in service were now converted to carry cargo. Pictured at Manchester Airport on a regular cargo service in July 1990 is Boeing 707-336C VR-HKK c/n 20517 of Air Hong Kong. The -300 series was the long-range intercontinental variant, with more of these being produced than any other. Air Hong Kong is still in business and this airframe was sold on to various carriers. It was later stored in Khartoum, Sudan, in 2009 and withdrawn from use the following year.

Seen leaving El Dorado International Airport, Bogotá, Colombia, is Boeing 707-324C HK-3604X c/n 19352 in November 1992. It is operated by Medellin-based TAMPA (Transportes Aéreos Merchantiles Panamericanos), an all-cargo airline. They are now part of the Avianca group, and this aircraft was sold to a company in Brazil where it was eventually withdrawn from use in December 2007 and broken up.

Pictured in September 1997 at Eloy Alfaro Air Base, Manta, Ecuador, is Boeing 707-321C HC-BGP c/n 19273 operated by AECA (Aeroservicios Ecuatorianos CA), who were based at Guayaquil. The large freight door is seen in the open position. The airline suspended its operations during 2000 and the aircraft was stored in Cotopaxi, Ecuador, and then broken up.

Miami International Airport has always been a hot bed of cargo operations from both South and Central America, as well as the Caribbean region. Pictured landing in April 1994 is Boeing 707-327C CC-CYA c/n 19530 of Chilean carrier LADECO (Línea Aérea de Cobra). The company was taken over and merged into LAN Chile, whilst this aircraft was sold on to a carrier in Eastern Europe to operate in Romania. It was withdrawn from use there in the early part of 1997.

Seen in the cargo area of Miami International Airport, In April 1994, is Boeing 707-330C PT-TCM c/n 19317 operated by AeroBrazil Cargo. Based at São Paulo, this airline later became part of Trans Brazil. This aircraft was sold on and re-registered to BETA (Brazilian Express Transportes Aéreos). The aircraft was damaged beyond economic repair following an accident on take-off at Eduardo Gomes International Airport, Manaus, Brazil, in October 2004. As the pilots of the 707 applied power to take off and released the brakes, a loud bang sounded. The pilots wisely made the decision to abandon the take-off roll and pulled back the power on all four Pratt & Whitney JT3D-3B engines. The aircraft turned slowly to the right-hand side. It later transpired that the main landing gear on the right-hand side of the aircraft had punctured through the lower part of the wing.

With a typically cloudy Miami background, Boeing 707-323C CP-1698 c/n 19586 of LAB Cargo (Lloyd Aéreo Boliviano Cargo) lands in October 1998. The Bolivian flag carrier ceased operations of both passenger and cargo services in 2010. By that time, this aircraft had been sold on to a company in Brazil. It was withdrawn from use at São Paulo in June 2009 and, in April of the following year, it was broken up.

Some cargo operators had little regard for the exterior appearance of their aircraft, whilst others made great efforts. An example of the latter are the cargo planes from Aerolineas Uruguayas (Aero Uruguay). Pictured arriving at Miami International Airport in April 1994, in a most attractive livery, is Boeing 707-331C CX-BPL c/n 19435. Sadly, the airline suspended its operations at the end of that year. The aircraft was sold on and subsequently operated by FIA (First International Airlines), a Belgian-based company, who had the aircraft registered in Aruba. Unfortunately, during its time with FIA, the aircraft was damaged beyond economic repair. The incident happened at Kananga Airport in the Democratic Republic of the Congo in January 1997. When the 707 landed, the left-hand side undercarriage leg collapsed, causing the aircraft to run off the side of the runway and catch fire. Thankfully, all of the crew escaped.

To disprove the idea that all 707s were used for cargo during the 1990s, Boeing 707-347C OD-AGV c/n 19967 is pictured landing at London Heathrow in September 1993. It is operating a scheduled passenger service for MEA (Middle East Airways), based in Beirut. The interior was configured for 18 first class passengers and 134 economy. The airline, which started in 1945, continues to operate to this day. However, the aircraft was sold to a company in Egypt and operated in an all-economy and combi-cargo mode. It moved later to Nigeria in the same role, before being withdrawn from use in Lagos and later broken up.

During the mid-1950s, the Boeing Company saw the need to develop a medium-range, jet-powered airliner with the ability to operate out of smaller airports with minimal ground support equipment. The first prototype Boeing 727 took to the air on 9 February 1963. Boeing had planned as much commonality with the 707 in order to save costs and cut down the risk of possible delays. The power plants selected for the new design were three Pratt & Whitney JT8D-7 turbofans, with two mounted on the side of the rear fuselage and the third below the fin. The first carrier to put the new Boeing 727-100 series into service was Eastern Air Lines on 1 February 1964, when it flew from their Miami International Airport base to Philadelphia and Washington DC. Pictured in March 1997 at Sharjah International Airport, United Arab Emirates (UAE), is Boeing 727-113C YA-FAU c/n 20343 of Ariana Afghan Airlines. It was being loaded with hundreds of cassette recorders. The Kabul-based flag carrier is still in operation. However, this aircraft, which was pristine upon acquisition, came to an unfortunate end. It was destroyed by the United States' bombing of Kabul Airport in October 2001, as an act of retaliation for the attacks on New York on 11 September 2001.

Photographed in September 1997 at Guayaquil, Ecuador, is Boeing 727-22 OB-1548 c/n 19152 of Aeroperú (Empresa de Transporte Aéreo del Perú), who were based in the capital, Lima. It was equipped for passengers and was configured with all-economy seating for 129 people. In March 1999, the airline ceased all its operations and this 727 was sold on, stored and eventually withdrawn from use in 2006 in Malabo, Equatorial Guinea.

Pictured in Miami International Airport, in October 1998, Boeing 727-23F HP-1229-PFC c/n 18429 has been converted for cargo operations and operated by Pacific International Airlines. Based at Tocumen International Airport, Panama City, the company suspended its operations during 2000 and this aircraft was sold on to a company in Africa. It was withdrawn from use in December 2005 and later broken up in Luanda, Angola.

The early generation of jets had problems with noise. This was a difficult problem especially for cargo and small parcel carriers, who often opted to fly their services during night-time hours and caused many complaints from people living near an airport. To solve this, the Boeing 727-100QF was developed; the 'QF' stands for 'Quiet Freighter'. The original P&W power plants were replaced by a trio of Rolls-Royce Tay 651/54 turbofans that were compliant with Stage 3 noise conditions and much more fuel efficient. Pictured in April 1994 at Orlando International Airport, Florida, is Boeing 727QF-173C N938UP c/n 19506. It is operated by UPS (United Parcel Services), who are today one of the giants of worldwide small parcel delivery operations. This 727 was permanently withdrawn from use in Roswell, New Mexico, in February 2008 and later broken up. A point of note about the new, quieter variant was the shape of the centre engine; it has a distinctive hump when compared to the standard 727.

All popular airliners are soon found to be too small for their operators, and so it was for the Boeing 727-100 series. The answer from the company was to fit two 10ft (3.05M) fuselage sections – one in front and the other behind the wings. This gave it a seating capacity of up to 189 people and was named the -200 series. The Pratt & Whitney JT8D engines were replaced with the -11, giving the aircraft more thrust. The first -200 flew on 27 July 1967; it went on to be the best-selling airliner of its day with 1258 -200s and 574 -100s sold, giving a grand total of 1832 airframes.

Pictured moving into its gate at Manchester Airport's Terminal Two, in June 1996, is Boeing 727-2D3 G-BPND c/n 21021 of London Gatwick-based Sabre Airways. The aircraft had a seating capacity of 187, and its role was holiday charter flights to the sun spots of the Mediterranean. The airline had been founded in 1994 and in 2000 was renamed Excell Airways. This 727 was sold on and initially stored in Goodyear, Arizona, in September 2006. It was then withdrawn from use at the end of the following year.

Mahfooz Aviation was based in the Saudi Arabian city of Jeddah, with its aircraft registered in Banjul, the Republic of the Gambia. Pictured in March 1997 at Sharjah International Airport, UAE, is Boeing 727-228 C5-DMB c/n 20411. It had just been painted and was pushed out of the SAIF Aviation Services hangar to bask in the hot sunshine. It was configured for passengers and had a capacity of 152 people. This aircraft was withdrawn from use in Addis Ababa, Ethiopia, in June 2002. While Mahfooz Aviation has no current aircraft registered to it, it plans to resume operation in due course.

Some airlines have very attractive colour schemes; one such was Caracas-based Venezuelan carrier, Servivensa. Photographed in November 1992 at El Dorado International Airport, Bogotá, is Boeing 727-2M7 YV-768C c/n 21457. The airline was part of the Avensa Group and they suspended passenger services in 2003. This 727 made its way to an African operator. In May 2003, it made a heavy landing at the Nigerian capital of Abuja. Later, it was stored at Kaduna and there it was reduced to spare parts to keep other 727s in the air.

Seen in late evening sunshine, in June 1998, at Helsinki Airport, Finland, is Boeing 727-287F OY-SEW c/n 21688, in the livery of small parcel company TNT. Based in Liege, Belgium, TNT International Aviation Services – now a subsidiary of FedEx (Federal Express) – had an amalgam of various European-registered aircraft in their fleet mix. This aircraft was stored in Tucson, Arizona, in June 2002 and permanently withdrawn from use at the end of the following year.

Miami Air International started operations with 727s in 1991. Seen at their base in Miami International Airport, in November 1992, is Boeing 727-225 N804MA c/n 22435. They operated passenger charter flights for cruise companies, professional sports teams, and the US military. Operations were suspended in May 2020. This aircraft had been sold to a Canadian operator and then permanently withdrawn from use in Hamilton, Ontario, at the end of 2008.

Pictured at East Midlands Airport, in July 1997, is Boeing 727-230 TC-ALM c/n 20431 of Air Alpha. The airline was based at Istanbul Airport and this aircraft was configured for 167 passengers in one class. They closed their operations in December 2001 and, subsequently, became Alpha Airlines. However, within a year, they had again ceased flying. This 727 was withdrawn at this location, the month this picture was taken, and used by the airport fire service for various training and rescue operations.

SAETA (Sociedad Anónima Ecuatoriana de Transportes Aéreos SA) was based at Mariscal Sucre International Airport, Quito. Pictured at Miami International Airport, in November 1992, is Boeing 727-282 HC-BRG c/n 20973. The company suspended its passenger services in February 2000 and this aircraft was stored at Guayaquil, Ecuador, before being broken up in 2007.

The flag carrier for Ecuador used to be Ecuatoriana (Empresa Ecuatoriana de Aviación). Seen in September 1997 at Mariscal Sucre International Airport, Quito, is Boeing 727-287 HC-BVT c/n 22603. The airline suspended all services between September 1993 and August 1995; they returned to the air in June 1996 following a takeover by Brazilian carrier VASP (Viação Aérea São Paulo). However, all operations ended when the new entity closed in 2006. This 727 was sold to a company in the United States and later withdrawn from use in Tucson, Arizona. It was then donated to a local community college for training purposes.

Pictured in September 1997 at Mariscal Sucre International Airport, Quito, is Boeing 727-2T3 HC-BHM – FAE 078 (the aircraft's air force serial) c/n 22078 of TAME (Transportes Aéreos Militares Ecuadorianos). The company was a branch of the nation's air force; its role was to operate services that would not be economic for a commercial airline, yet provided a vital link for the large country. By 2011, they ceased to be part of the air force and were an independent carrier, and in May 2020 all services were suspended. This 727 was withdrawn from use at its Quito base in June 2009.

Another airline with a very smart livery was Air Columbus. Seen landing at Manchester Airport, in April 1991, is Boeing 727-2J4 CS-TKB c/n 20764. The company was a holiday charter operator, flying passengers to their base at Funchal, Madeira. It operated the aircraft in an all-economy configuration for 178 passengers and they were associated with the Danish carrier Stirling Airways. Operations were closed in 1994 and this aircraft was sold to an American operator. It was first stored in Marana, Arizona, in 2002 and then broken up in February 2004.

Mexicana (Mexicana de Aviacíon) was one of the oldest airlines in the world, with a history dating back as far as 1921. Pictured landing at Miami International Airport, in October 1998, is Boeing 727-264 XA-MEL c/n 22413. It is always sad when a carrier with such a long pedigree closes down, and Mexicana's closure in August 2010 was no exception. This 727 has a happier tale as it was re-registered as XC-FPA and joined the national federal police, where it serves to this day.

Seen on the move at Beijing, China, in October 1999, is Boeing 727-281 JU-1037 c/n 20573 of MIAT (Mongolian Airlines). Based in the Mongolian capital of Ulaanbaatar, MIAT still operates as the nation flag carrier. This aircraft was sold to an operator in South Africa; it was later stored in Johannesburg, in December 2007, and permanently withdrawn from use a year later.

It is surprising to learn that the first variant of what went on to be, for many years, the best-selling airliner in the world, only had an initial production run of 30 airframes. This was the Boeing 737-100 series. The short-haul, jet-powered airliner was a logical field for the company to enter, as they had best-sellers with the long-range 707 and medium-range 727. The Boeing Company's first plans were for an aircraft with some 50 to 60 seats. However, the launch customer, the West German flag carrier, Lufthansa, wanted more capacity when they placed the first order for 21 aircraft in February 1965. To accommodate this customer, the fuselage was lengthened to accommodate a seating plan for at least 100 passengers.

On 9 April 1967, the first 737-100 took to the air from the Boeing Field and landed at Paine Field, Seattle. The first revenue service took place on 10 February 1968, and the power plants for the aircraft were a pair of Pratt & Whitney JT8D-7 turbojets with an output of 14,000lb st. Pictured on the ramp at its base at Phoenix Sky Harbor International Airport, in October 1998, is Boeing 737-112 N708AW c/n 19771, operated by America West Airlines. It also has the name *Phoenix Suns,* after the Arizona-based basketball team who used the aircraft to fly the team around the country. It was withdrawn from use in Opa Locka, Florida, in January 2000, and broken up. America West Airlines later merged with US Airways and, despite being the dominant partner in the merger, took the US Airways name.

Despite only making 30 airframes, the 737-100 was operated by 20 different companies. One such was Lima, Peru-based Aero Continente. Pictured at base, in September 1997, is Boeing 737-130 P4-ASB (later OB-1736) c/n 19017; this aircraft was put into store at Lima. This carrier started in May 1992 and suspended operations late in 2001. It restarted in 2003, but owing to alleged illegal activities it lost its operating certificate in 2004. It was later bought out by its staff and resumed services, only to have the authorities revoke its certificate once again in 2005.

Since most potential carrier companies thought the -100 series too small for their needs, the Boeing Company announced the -200 series. It was longer by 78in (1.93m) and could seat up to 130 people. The first order was from United States' domestic giant United Airlines, who wanted 40. Both versions were built concurrently and United Airlines began revenue services with the -200 in April 1968, only two months after Lufthansa had with the -100. Pictured landing at London Gatwick, in August 1998, is Boeing 737-230 EI-CNY c/n 22113 of Irish low-cost carrier Ryanair. It is painted as a flying billboard for 'Kilkenny, the Cream of Irish Beers' – note how the cockpit has the white head of the drink. It was one of several aircraft that the airline used to advertise products or companies. This aircraft was sold on and currently serves with Venezuelan RUTACA Airlines.

Air Great Wall deserves to be classed as the perfect name for a Chinese airline. This carrier was based in the city of Ningbo and, in 2002, were taken over and merged into China Eastern Airlines. Pictured on a service to Beijing, in October 1999, is Boeing 737-2T4 B-2507 c/n 23273. This aircraft is currently with a carrier in the Sudan, but in store.

Pictured landing at Miami International Airport, in October 1998, is Boeing 737-201 N247US c/n 22754 of MetroJet. Formed in June 1998, MetroJet were a division of US Airways that offered low cost and low fares. The interior was a one-class 118 seat configuration. The division was closed in 2001. This 737 was sold to an operator in the Lebanon and put into store.

COPA Airlines (Compania Panamena de Aviacíon) are the flag carrier for Panama and have a history dating back to 1944. They operate to over 30 nations in the Americas and Caribbean region. Seen lining up for take-off at Miami International Airport, in October 1998, is Boeing 737-230C HP-1134-CMP c/n 20253. This aircraft was sold to a company in Colombia in 2000 and later withdrawn from use and broken up.

Seen at Phoenix, Arizona, in October 1998, is Boeing 737-201 N217US c/n 20215 of Denver, Colorado-based Frontier Airlines – Spirit of the West. Their fleet of -200 series aircraft are fitted out with 108 all-economy seats and every aircraft has, on each side of the fin, a picture of an animal or bird. An eagle can be seen on the pictured aircraft, and a mountain lion adorns the other side. Frontier still operates today. However, this aircraft was sold to a carrier in Peru, stored in August 2001 and withdrawn from use and broken up for spare parts by 2004.

The UK flag carrier, British Airways (BA), has operated every Boeing airliner except the 727 (although a South African franchise operator did fly the 727 in BA livery). In June 1997, BA unveiled a new company colour scheme in which the tails of the aircraft would be designed by artists from all around the world. The outcome of this redesign was divisive, and the designs were both loved or hated in equal measure. After two years, the project was abandoned. Pictured landing at Manchester Airport, in April 1998, is Boeing 737-236 G-BGDT c/n 21807. This tail is *Animals and Trees* by Cg'ose Ntcox'o, an artist from the Ncoakhoe tribe of San people who live in the Kalahari Desert of Botswana. This aircraft was sold on to an operator in Pakistan and, by 2012, had been withdrawn for use.

Transaero Airlines started operating in November 1991 and were, notably, the first non-Aeroflot airline approved for scheduled services, shortly before the official fall of the USSR. They were also one of the first of the newly formed Russian carriers to adopt mainly Western-built aircraft. They suspended services in October 2015. Seen in September 1995 at their base in Sheremetyevo International Airport, Moscow, is Boeing 737-236 YL-BAC c/n 22034. This leased aircraft was withdrawn at the company base at the end of 2002.

Since the Boeing 737-200 was a great success, the logical progression was to improve it. The 737-300 first flew in February 1984. It was longer by 44in (1.11m) forward and 60in (1.52m) aft of the wing, with extended wingtips. The biggest change was a completely new power plant – a CFM-56 with a thrust of 22,100lb st. The shape of the new nacelle to hold the engine had to change from rounded to more oval shaped, as there would otherwise not have been sufficient ground clearance. Pictured at Manchester Airport, in May 1996, is Boeing 737-375 EC-GFU c/n 23808 of Spanish holiday charter operator, Air Europa. This carrier still operates to this day, and this aircraft was stored at Bournemouth, United Kingdom, in 2001 and then broken up.

Pictured landing at London Heathrow, in June 1996, is Boeing 737-332 EZ-A002 c/n 25994 of Turkmenistan Airlines. At that time, the newly formed airline, which was now the flag carrier for the previous USSR republic, operated just a small number of Western-built aircraft within the large fleet of Soviet-era airframes. The airline continues to operate and this aircraft was last reported as stored in Craiova, Romania.

Beginning operations in May 1998, Go Fly was launched by British Airways as a low-cost subsidiary. It was intended to operate a wide range of European scheduled services. Landing at their base at London Stansted, in August 1999, is Boeing 737-3Y0 G-IGOG c/n 23927. In 2002, Go Fly were taken over by easyJet; this aircraft was sold on to a company in the Republic of Guinea and was in store by 2014.

Chinese carrier Shenzhen Airlines is based in the city of the same name. Its main operations are in the south of the country, providing services to the Shenzhen Special Economic Zone (SEZ). Seen arriving at its gate at Beijing, in October 1999, is Boeing 737-3K9 B-2933 c/n 25788. At that time, they had an all-737 fleet, but it is now a mix with Airbus single-aisle aircraft. This aircraft was withdrawn from use in 2012.

Delta Air Regionalflugverkehr began operations in 1978. However, after its majority purchase by British Airways in 1992, their name was changed to Deutsche BA. They became a low-cost carrier and, in 2003, the name was again changed, this time to dba. Seen at London Gatwick, in March 1997, is Boeing 737-3L9 D-ADBB c/n 26440. This aircraft was sold on to several carriers and is now with one in Thailand but in store.

Dallas, Texas-based Southwest Airlines are the textbook operator that so many start-ups try to emulate when it comes to running a low-cost, no-frills airline. Pictured at Phoenix Sky Harbor International Airport, in October 1998, is Boeing 737-3H4 N352SW c/n 24888. It is one of their fleet painted in a special livery, designed to show off the 'Lone Star' state of Texas. This aircraft was withdrawn from use in Tucson, Arizona, and parted out for spares.

Whilst they have become common today, few 737s were seen as cargo aircraft in the 1990s. Lined up to take off at Miami International Airport, in April 1994, is Boeing 737-3S3F N841LF c/n 23811 operated by Aviateca (Empresa Guatemalteca de Aviación SA). This company was later amalgamated into the TACA group of airlines. This aircraft is currently with a company in Malaysia.

British airline Dan-Air took its name from the shipping brokers Davies and Newman, who formed it in 1953. They operated both holiday charters and scheduled services. They were taken over by British Airways for the sum of just £1 following mounting debts, and their last service was in November 1992. Pictured landing at Manchester Airport, in March 1991, is Boeing 737-3Q8 G-BNNJ c/n 24068. This aircraft was sold on to a company in the United States, and withdrawn from use in Tucson, Arizona, in 2016 and broken up.

British low-cost airline easyJet has grown to be one of the largest carriers in Europe, with aircraft based in many cities around the continent. Operations began from their London Luton Airport base in 1995. Pictured at their first international destination, Amsterdam Airport Schiphol, In August 1997, is Boeing 737-3Y0 G-EZYC c/n 24462. Note that, in this picture, the company telephone number for bookings is in large letters on the fuselage while, today, this has been replaced by the website address. This is an interesting touchstone for technological developments over the last two decades – in 1997, the telephone was the most common way to book, as many people did not yet own their own computer. The company has now an all-Airbus fleet, whist this 737 is currently with a South African company as a cargo aircraft.

The first 737-400 flew in February 1988. Once again, the fuselage was extended by 66in (1.67m) forward and 48in (1.21m) aft of the wing. It could now hold up to 168 passengers, depending upon the airline's configuration. Pictured in November 1999 at Don Mueang, Bangkok, Thailand's then main airport, is leased Boeing 737-4H6 9M-MMH c/n 27084 operated by Myanmar Airways International (MAI). Based in Yangon, they were formed in 1993 to operate international services to Bangkok, Singapore and Kuala Lumpur using two leased Malaysian registered aircraft. While the company continues its services, this aircraft was withdrawn from use in 2013 and stored.

Seen at its base at East Midlands Airport, in September 1998, is Boeing 737-4Y0 G-OBMG c/n 23870 in the livery of British Midland Airways. The company had a history dating back to 1938 and, following World War Two, operated as Derby Airways. In July 1964, the company took its present name, and in October 2012, they were purchased by British Airways. This aircraft was sold on and had several operators before being broken up.

Turkey has a large tourist industry with many airlines bringing in passengers from all over Europe. One such is Pegasus Airlines, which operates both holiday charter and scheduled flights. Once an exclusively 737 operator, these aircraft are in the process of being replaced by Airbus A320/321 aircraft. Pictured at Liverpool Airport, approaching to line up on runway 27, is Boeing 737-4Y0 TC-AFK c/n 24684. This aircraft is now in service with the Indonesian Air Force.

When the -500 variant of the 737 arrived, it did not follow the pattern of enlargement. Instead, the Boeing Company returned this aircraft almost to the size of the 737-200 in fuselage, coming in at just 19in (47cm) more in length. Nevertheless, it did have extended wingtips and a modernised cockpit instrumentation. It first flew in June 1989. The reason for the size contraction was that some airlines found the -300 and -400 too large for their needs and wanted the size of the -200, but with the advantages of the later models. Pictured at Frankfurt Airport, in June 1997, is Boeing 737-55D SP-LKE c/n 27130 of national flag carrier LOT (Polish Airlines). Based in Warsaw, they were originally formed in 1929. This aircraft is currently operated by an airline in Mexico.

Following the -500 series came the 'new generation' of 737s. The fin height was increased, and the wingspan was grown by 17ft 8in (5.43m). The pilots were also presented with technologically advanced 'glass cockpits'. There were three planned versions; the -600 to replace the -500; the -700 to replace the -300; the -800 to replace the -400. All would retain the CFM-56 power plant, albeit with slightly different thrust settings. Pictured at Zürich Airport, in August 1998, is Boeing 737-7Q8 HB-IIH c/n 28209 of Basel-based TEA Switzerland. The carrier commenced operations – mainly holiday charters flights – in March 1989. In 1999, they were taken over by easyJet and renamed easyJet Switzerland, now with an all-Airbus fleet. This aircraft is currently with an airline in the United States.

Based in the Chinese holiday island of the same name, Hainan Airlines began services in May 1993. Today, they operate across that vast nation. Pictured arriving at its gate, in October 1999, at Beijing, is Boeing 737-86N B-2637 c/n 28576. This 737 is listed as being in store in the state of Arizona, following the lease to a Korean airline.

Without a doubt, the Boeing 747 was a game changer, both for the airlines of the world and for the millions of passengers who now were able to afford to travel long-haul. It had entered service with Pan American Airways (Pan Am) at the start of 1970. By the 1990s, there were five versions in service of what became known as the 'jumbo jet'. Pictured at its Dublin base, in June 1994, is Boeing 747-148 EI-ASI c/n 19744 of Irish flag carrier Aer Lingus. This aircraft was sold on and stored in Roswell, New Mexico, in 2000 and then broken up three years later.

Seen landing at Athens International Airport, in June 1993, is Boeing 747-130 N603FF c/n 19746 of New York-based Tower Air. They flew passenger charters and scheduled services as well as cargo. Operations were suspended in May 2000. This ex-Lufthansa airframe was withdrawn at their base and broken up, with the registration being cancelled in 2001.

In April 1971, the 747 entered passenger service with Air Canada. It began with a domestic, albeit long, flight from Toronto to Vancouver, followed two months later by services to London. Pictured landing at London Heathrow, in July 1995, is Boeing 747-133 C-FTOC c/n 20015. They operated the early 747s for three more years. This aircraft was sold on in 1998, then withdrawn and stored in Opa Locka, Florida, and broken up the following year.

British Airways' (BA) 747s did not start revenue services until April 1971, despite the first three aircraft being delivered up to a year prior. This was because of industrial action by the flight deck crew. At that time, they were still known as BOAC (British Overseas Airways Corporation) and did not become BA until the end of March 1974. Seen arriving at their base at London Heathrow, in October 1993, is Boeing 747-136 G-AWNC c/n 19763. This aircraft was stored in 1998, sold on the following year to a carrier in the Middle East and eventually withdrawn from use in Marana, Arizona, in 2000. It was scrapped five years later.

The -200 variant of the 747 followed on quickly, with its first flight on 11 October 1970. It had a strengthened airframe and an increased fuel capacity. Customers could also choose an engine option from Pratt & Whitney, Rolls-Royce and General Electric, all of whom offered power plants. Pictured at Miami International Airport, in October 1998, is Boeing 747-2F6B N534MC c/n 21832 of Atlas Air. This aircraft had been delivered to Atlas Air, who continue to operate, a few months earlier and was converted to a freighter. Sold on to several United States-based customers, it was stored in 2012 and then broken up.

The 'flying billboard' form of advertising is very popular. Seen at Bangkok, in November 1999, is Boeing 747-243B I-DEMS c/n 22969 of Italian flag carrier Alitalia. It is painted in a striking aluminium finish to advertise Bulgari watches. This aircraft was bought new and stayed with Alitalia for the full duration of its service life. It left the fleet in July 2002, was stored in the United States and broken up in Marana, Arizona, in March 2007.

Pictured arriving at its gate in Frankfurt Airport, in June 1997, is Boeing 747-281B JA8181 c/n 23698 of Japanese carrier All Nippon Airways (ANA), one of that nation's two main international airlines. Upon selling, it was converted to cargo configuration and, when registered to an airline in Armenia, was damaged beyond economic repair following a landing and runway excursion at Abuja Airport, Nigeria, in December 2013.

Arriving at its home base of Athens International Airport, in June 1993, is Boeing 747-212B SX-OAE c/n 21935 of Olympic Airways. At the time, they were state owned. However, following large debts, they are now a private company operating as Olympic Air. This aircraft was withdrawn from use in 2000 and is in store.

Owned by the Iranian Air Force, SAHA Airlines started operations in 1990, suspended them in 2013 and began again in 2017. Seen in March 1997 at Sharjah International Airport, UAE, is Boeing 747-259F EP-SHH (5-8114 air force serial) c/n 21487. As can be seen in this picture, the company name does not appear on the aircraft; only the word 'cargo' appears, indicating its role. This aircraft is currently with the Iranian Air Force.

Dubai, UAE, is a major cargo hub because of its location between Europe and Asia. Photographed landing there, in March 1997, is Boeing 747-254F HL7474 c/n 22169 operated by Korean Air Cargo, which is part of the flag carrier for South Korea. This aircraft was sold on and stored in Filton, United Kingdom, at the start of 2008 and broken up in September 2012.

The -300 variant of the 747 first flew in October 1982. The design mirrored a basic -200 variant, with the addition of a stretched upper deck; again, the customers had a choice of the three major engine manufacturers. Arriving at Bangkok, in November 1999, is Boeing 747-338 VH-EBT c/n 23222 of Australia's flag carrier, Qantas Airways Limited (Queensland and Northern Territory Aerial Services). This aircraft was named *City of Wagga Wagga*, stored at the start of 2007, and was broken up three years later. The -300 variant was the last of what were called the 'classic' 747s.

The -400 variant of the 747 was a giant leap in performance. This was due, in part, to several major airlines coming together to talk to Boeing about their current and future needs. This group included KLM (Koninklijke Luchtvaart Maatschappij), Qantas Airways Limited, British Airways, Singapore Airlines and Cathay Pacific Airways – all major 747 users. The new aircraft now had an advanced 'glass cockpit' with digital avionics, the need for only two pilots and no flight engineer. The first aircraft flew in April 1998, and February the following year saw Northwest Airlines, the launch customer, operate the first revenue service. A major point of recognition were the winglets on this version, added to extend range and reduce fuel burn in a long, high altitude cruise. The only models not fitted with these are the Japanese domestic ones, who only operate over relatively short distances. Pictured lining up on runway 28 at Zürich Airport, in August 1998, Boeing 747-4R7F LX-FCV c/n 25866 is making a very tight turn to land on runway 32. It is operated by Cargolux Airlines International, an all-cargo carrier based in Luxembourg. This aircraft is currently with a United States parcel carrier.

On the move at Frankfurt Airport, in June 1997, is Boeing 747-48E HL7423 c/n 25782 of Asiana Airlines, the second largest carrier in Korea. This aircraft was configured to hold 12 first class, 32 business and 236 economy passengers. It was powered by the General Electric CF-6 engine. It is still in service with the company, but it has been converted to a freighter.

Based in Taiwan, China Airlines are the largest carrier in the Republic of China. Despite being separate from the communist government in Beijing, both countries share the same registration letter of 'B'. Arriving at its gate at Bangkok, Thailand, in November 1999, is Boeing 747-409 B-18205 c/n 28712. This aircraft was put into store in San Bernardino, California, in 2017 and was to be parted out for spare parts.

The oddest variant of the 747 was the -SP (Special Performance). It was to fill the gap between the single-aisle 707 and the twin-aisle 747, as well as compete with the Douglas DC-10 and Lockheed L1011 TriStar. The length was reduced by 48ft (14.63m) and it had a substantial range of nearly 7,000 miles (11,265km). It first took to the sky in July 1975. Pictured in July 1997 at London Heathrow is Boeing 747SP-44 ZS-SPC c/n 21134, operated by Air Namibia. The airline was based in the Namibian capital, Windhoek, until February 2021 when the government closed the carrier owing to mounting debts. This aircraft was on lease from SAA (South African Airways), hence the registration; it was retired later that year and then spent some time in store. In 2006, it was donated to the South African Airways Museum Society and can be found on display at Rand Airport, Johannesburg.

SAA were the second largest operator of the Boeing -SP model, having six. It suited their needs well. When they purchased these models in the 1970s, the country was still under the apartheid rules of the white minority government and they were not allowed to operate into most African nations. The ultra-long range of the -SP meant that they could fly non-stop to Europe or the United States, thus widening the potential operations for this airline. Seen on tow at Amsterdam Airport Schiphol, in August 1997, is Boeing 747SP-44 ZS-SPE c/n 21254. It was withdrawn from service in October 2003 in Johannesburg and broken up five years later. It did, however, provide parts for the -SP being preserved at Rand Airport, Johannesburg. The production run of the type was just 45 models. A very small number still operate as engine test beds and one is used by NASA as a flying telescope.

The Boeing 727 was the first jet airliner to pass the 1,000 mark in sales, but all good things come to an end. Eventually, a replacement would be needed in the medium-range field. The aircraft we know as the 757 was rolled out at the Boeing factory in Renton, Washington, in January 1982. The first flight taking place the following month. It was the first American airliner launched with a foreign engine. As the first customers were British Airways and Eastern Air Lines, the selected power plant was the British-made Rolls-Royce RB-211-535. Also on offer was the Pratt & Whitney PW 2037 engine. The 757-200 version (there was no -100) started revenue services on the first day of 1983, with Eastern Air Lines. On the move at Phoenix Sky Harbor Airport, in October 1998, is Boeing 757-2S7 N904AW c/n 23566 operated by America West. It is in special livery to advertise the local baseball team, the Arizona Diamondbacks. This aircraft was put in storage in 2016.

Seen at Frankfurt Airport, in June 1997, is Boeing 757-2G5 EC-EFX c/n 23118. LTE International Airways were a Spanish holiday charter carrier that was, in part, founded by German-based LTU airline. The airline was rebranded Volar Air and later suspended services in November 2008. This aircraft was stored in 2004 and broken up in Opa Locka, Florida.

Pictured being pushed back from Terminal One at Manchester Airport, in May 1998, in the company of a sister ship, is Boeing 757-225 G-RJGR c/n 22197 of local Airtours International Airways (later MyTravel Airways). This aircraft was broken up in Marana, Arizona, in 2006.

Pictured climbing out of its Ürümqi Diwopu International Airport base in the far west of China, in October 1999, is Boeing 757-2Y0 B-2827 c/n 26156 of China Xinjiang Airlines. The carrier was absorbed by China Southern Airlines in November 2004. This aircraft was first stored, and then converted to a freighter that now serves with China Postal Airlines.

United Airlines are one of the current giants of the United States' market. Seen in November 1992 in Simón Bolívar International Airport, Caracas, in November 1992 is Boeing 757-222 N545UA c/n 25323. It was put into store in October 2015.

The 757 has proved to be a very popular aircraft for many of the United Kingdom's holiday charter companies. Seen at Newcastle International Airport, in May 1997, is Boeing 757-25F G-FCLD c/n 28718 in the livery of Flying Colours Airlines (FCA). After being purchased by Thomas Cook & Son in 1998, FCA was merged with another Thomas Cook-owned airline, Caledonian Airways, to form JMC Airlines. This aircraft was stored in 2014, converted to a freighter, and now operates in India.

Boeing 757-225 G-OOOV c/n 22211 heads a line of four sister ships at Terminal Two at Manchester Airport in June 1996. It is in the livery of Air 2000, which was a British holiday charter company with bases at Manchester Airport and London Gatwick. Like so many airlines, they had a name change; in April 2004, they were rebranded as First Choice Airways. This aircraft was converted to a freighter, served in the Middle East, and was put in store in the United States in June 2017.

On the move in March 1997, at Sharjah International Airport, UAE, is Boeing 757-2Y0 SE-DUL c/n 26151 operated by Blue Scandinavia. It had called in for a refuelling stop on its way to Phuket in Thailand. Blue Scandinavia was the new name for the charter division of Transwede Leisure, which had been split and sold in 1996 to Fritidsresor. In 1998, Fritidsresor was purchased by Thomson Travel and, following TUI Group's purchase of Thomson in 2000, was rebranded as TUI fly Nordic in 2005. This aircraft was converted to a freighter and serves with an American parcel delivery company.

Landing at Miami International Airport, in April 1994, is Boeing 757-2Y0 EI-CEZ c/n 26154 leased by Colombian flag carrier Avianca. This carrier continues to operate, albeit with many changes of management and ownership. This leased aircraft was put into store in 2010, converted to a freighter and serves in that role today.

Boeing stretched the 757 by 13ft 3in (4.03m) forward and 9ft 9in aft of the wing. The first one flew in August 1998, and the launch customer was Condor, the largest German holiday charter operator and a subsidiary of Lufthansa. This new variant was the 757-300. Arriving at Condor's Frankfurt base, in June 1999, is Boeing 757-330 D-ABOE c/n 29012. Despite being a holiday airline, the aircraft is configured with 48 business class and 217 economy seats. It still serves with the company.

It may come as a surprise to some, but the Boeing 767 came before the 757. Its first flight was in September 1981 and it was one of the first twin-engine, wide-body jets. All three major engine manufacturers, Pratt & Whitney (P&W), Rolls-Royce and General Electric were available to airline customers. The main competition was from Airbus, who had just launched their all-new A300. The launch customer was United Airlines (UA), who had the first revenue service on 8 September 1982; they flew from Chicago to Denver with a P&W powered aircraft. As with the 757, there was no -100 series. Pictured landing at Manchester Airport, in April 1991, is Boeing 767-204 G-BRIG c/n 24757 of UK holiday charter operator Britannia Airways, the first to operate the aircraft in Europe. The carrier was rebranded as Thomsonfly in September 2004 and then as TUI Airways. This aircraft is still flying passengers, but is now owned by an operator in Jordan.

Sweden, Denmark and Norway share a joint airline named SAS (Scandinavian Airlines System). This airline has bases in all three capitals and the aircraft are registered between all the three nations. Seen landing at London Heathrow, in September 1993, is Boeing 767-283ER LN-RCC c/n 24728. The -ER stands for 'Extended Range' and has extra fuel tanks fitted in the centre section. After its service with SAS, this aircraft spent most of its time in Latin America before being stored in 2015 and broken up two years later.

On the move at Amsterdam Airport Schiphol, in August 1997, is Boeing 767-2B1 PT-TAK c/n 25421 of TransBrazil. The carrier ceased operations at the end of 2001 and this aircraft moved across South America, in 1999, to Colombia. It went into store in 2011.

Boeing 767-2N0 Z-WPE c/n 24713 is pictured at Frankfurt Airport in June 1999. It is owned by flag carrier for the African nation, Air Zimbabwe, and has spent its entire life with this company. Today, it carries the name *Victoria Falls*.

Once one of the great names of American aviation, Trans World Airlines (TWA) were taken over by American Airlines in April 2001. Seen in their final livery at London Gatwick, in August 1997, is Boeing 767-231 N605TW c/n 22568. This aircraft was broken up in 2004.

It had become normal to stretch the fuselage length of a new Boeing airliner, and so it was with the 767. It was extended by a plug 10ft 1in (3.07m) forward and 11ft (3.35m) aft of the wing. The prototype of the 767-300 series first flew in January 1986, with Japan Airlines as the launch customer. Pictured on the move at Miami International Airport, in October 1998, is Boeing 767-361F CC-CZZ c/n 25756 operated by Lan Chile Cargo, having been delivered to the carrier the previous month. It is still in service with the company, although they have now been rebranded as LATAM Cargo Chile.

On pushback from its gate at Terminal One at Manchester Airport, in June 1996, is Boeing 767-3Y0 EC-FHA c/n 25000 of Spanish holiday charter operator Spanair. It was configured with 18 business and 248 economy seats. The Palma de Mallorca-based company suspended services in January 2012. This aircraft had been sold on in 2002 and operated in several countries before being put into store in 2014.

Seen at Manchester Airport, in May 1998, is Boeing 767-31A PH-MCI c/n 25312 of Dutch charter operator Martinair. They were a subsidiary of KLM and now fly as an all-cargo carrier. The configuration for passengers in this aircraft was 24 business and 248 economy seats. This aircraft was broken up in 2014, following period of storage.

Royal Brunei Airlines commenced operations in May 1975 and are the flag carrier of the small, yet very wealthy, nation of Brunei, Borneo. Seen arriving at London Heathrow, in September 1993, is Boeing 767-33A V8-RBG c/n 25532. This aircraft was in a three-class layout with 13 first, 28 business and 168 economy seats. It was stored in 2010 and sold the following year to an operator in the Ukraine. In 2013, it was stored once again and then broken up.

The Boeing Company felt it had need of an aircraft to fill the gap between the 747 and the 767. Competition for this middle ground came from Airbus in the form of the A330 and A340. The new Boeing aircraft evolved into the 777 – again, there was no -100 series. The launch customer was United Airlines (UA) with an order in 1990; the prototype flew in June 1994. It was the company's first fly-by-wire for the control systems; they were behind Airbus in this innovation. All three major engine manufacturers – Pratt & Whitney (P&W), Rolls-Royce (RR) and General Electric (GE) – could fit their products to the 777. Pictured at Beijing, in October 1999, is Boeing 777-228 F-GSPF c/n 29007 of Air France. This aircraft is powered by the General Electric GE90-94B engine and is in a three-class configuration with 12 first, 56 business, and 202 economy class seats. It still serves with Air France.

At the beginning of the 1990s, the sight of a Western-built aircraft in the colours of Russian flag carrier Aeroflot would have been unthinkable. They only operated Soviet-built aircraft. However, here, in October 1999, is Boeing 777-2Q8(ER) VP-BAS c/n 27607 on a service into Beijing. Their first Western design was the Airbus A310 that was put into service in 1992. To supplement their fleet of Russian wide-bodied aircraft, which included both the Ilyushin IL-86 and 96, in 1998 they added a pair of leased Boeing 777s. Powered by the General Electric GE90 engine, the aircraft were in a three-class configuration. Aeroflot had raised its standards a great deal to equal many Western airlines. This aircraft moved on to Vietnam Airlines and now serves with Austrian Airlines and carries the name *Blue Danube*.

In October 1997, the 777-300 saw its first flight. It had been stretched by the insertion of two plugs, one 17ft 5in (5.3m) forward and a second 15ft 8in (4.77m) aft of the wing. The first deliveries were to Cathay Pacific in May 1998. Pictured at Bangkok, in November 1999, is Boeing 777-312 9V-SYB c/n 28516 of Singapore Airlines. The company are one of the largest operators of the 777; they hold a fleet of over 50 aircraft of this model, all of which are powered by the Rolls-Royce Trent 892 engine. Like most carriers, Singapore Airlines utilised a three-class seating configuration. This aircraft was sold on to a Russian carrier, Transaero Airlines, in March 2012 and, following their collapse, it is now with Rossiya Airlines, Russia.

Following on from the French-designed Sud Aviation SE 210 Caravelle and the British-made BAC 1-11 (also written as the BAC One-Eleven) was the American-manufactured Douglas DC-9. It first flew in February 1965 and followed the European precedent of having a pair of rear-mounted engines – it used Pratt & Whitney JT8D-5 turbojets with an output of 12,000lb st. The fuselage had an overall length of 104ft 5in (31.82m). The launch customer was Delta Air Lines. Pictured in November 1992 at its hangar at its El Dorado International Airport base, Bogotá, is Douglas DC-9-15 HK-2865X c/n 45722 of Intercontinental Colombia. This original length variant was configured for 83 passengers. In September 2005, the company suspended services; this aircraft had been broken up, at base, in June the previous year.

The Douglas DC-9 was improved throughout its lifetime. Pictured at Zürich Airport, in August 1998, is Douglas DC-9-21 OY-KIA c/n 47301 of SAS (Scandinavian Airlines System).The DC-9-21 had its short-field performance improved by the addition of 24in (60.9cm) extensions to the wingtips and an improved Pratt & Whitney JT8D-9 engine. This aircraft had an unusual fate, it was first sold on to an airline in the United States and then to one in Latin America. It was broken up in 2008, but the cockpit was saved and used as a room in a hotel in Costa Rica.

The Douglas DC-9-31 was, essentially, a DC-9-21 with a fuselage stretch of 15ft (4.57m) that could now hold up to 115 passengers in a one-class layout. Pictured at Miami International Airport, in April 1994, is Douglas DC-9-31 P4-MDD c/n 47271 of Air Aruba. It was the flag carrier for the Netherland's constituent country of Aruba, located in the Caribbean. They suspended services in October 2000 and this aircraft was sold on and broken up in 2006.

The DC-9-32 had a heavier maximum take-off weight and could be fitted with higher thrust versions of the Pratt & Whitney JT8D engine. Pictured in April 1994 at Tampa International Airport, Florida, is Douglas DC-9-32 N902VJ c/n 47177 in the smart livery of ValuJet Airlines. Based in Atlanta, they had commenced operations in October 1993 and were merged into AirTran Airways in September 1997. This aircraft was withdrawn from service in 2002 and broken up in Opa Locka, Florida, and the registration cancelled in September 2003.

On the ramp at Las Américas International Airport, Santo Domingo, Dominican Republic, in November 1992 is Douglas DC-9-32 EC-BQT c/n 47446 of Spanish national airline Iberia. The aircraft was being used for regional operations. This DC-9 was sold to an Argentinian carrier and was destroyed in a crash, which was sadly fatal for all 74 people on board, in October 1997. It was on an internal flight from Posadas, Argentina, to the capital, Buenos Aires, when it encountered unexpected bad weather. This caused the crew to lose control and, following the deployment of the slats at too great a speed, it impacted into soft ground on the banks of the Uruguay River.

The DC-9-41 had an extension to the fuselage of 6ft 2in (1.88m) and could now house 125 passengers. Pictured at Miami International Airport, in April 1994, is Douglas DC-9-41 N759NW c/n 47287 of Minneapolis-based Northwest Airlines. In 2010, they were taken over and integrated into Delta Air Lines. This aircraft was withdrawn from use in 2010.

The next model of the DC-9, as expected, featured an increase in size; the DC-9-51 had a fuselage stretch of 8ft (2.43m) with passenger capacity increased to 139. Pictured in June 1998 at its base at Helsinki Airport, Finland, is Douglas DC-9-51 OH-LYP c/n 47696 in the colours of national airline Finnair. This aircraft was sold to a company in the Ukraine in 2004, and later put into store.

In April 1967, the Douglas Aircraft Company were taken over by McDonnell Aircraft to form McDonnell Douglas. However, it was some time into the life of the DC-9 that a new aircraft designation came into use. This was the MD-81, and it first flew in October 1979. Developed from the DC-9-51, it had an increase both forward and aft of the wing extension to the fuselage totalling 14ft 3in (4.34m). This brought the length of the aircraft to 147ft 10in (45.05m) and passenger capacity to 172. The cockpit instrumentation was also updated, the fuel capacity increased and wingspan stretched by 14ft (4.26m) with the flaps and slats modified. Seen at Zürich Airport, in August 1998, is McDonnell Douglas MD-81 Z3-ARB c/n 48046 of Avioimpex of Macedonia. It is worth noting that this nation was once a part of dissolved state of Yugoslavia. The carrier had its licence revoked by the local Civil Aviation Authority (CAA) in 2002 following growing debts and, consequently, this aircraft has been in store since 2003 in Victorville, California.

On the move to its gate at London Heathrow, in July 1993, is McDonnell Douglas MD-81 S5-ABE c/n 48046 of Ljubljana, Slovenia-based Adria Airways. Once again, it is notable that Slovenia was another country that came from the dissolved state of Yugoslavia. The carrier suspended operations when, in September 2019, it was declared bankrupt. Eagle-eyed readers will have spotted that this and the previous aircraft are the same airframe. This is because it moved across the region to join Avioimpex.

Pictured landing at Miami International Airport, in October 1998, is McDonnell Douglas MD-82 PJ-SEF c/n 49123 of ALM (Antillean Airlines), who were based in the Netherland constituency of Curacao. The MD-82 was equipped with Pratt & Whitney JT8D-217 turbofans with an output of 20,000lb st and designed for hot and high locations. The carrier was closed in 2001 and, in 2004, this aircraft was stored and subsequently broken up.

McDonnell Douglas' MD-83 replicated the size of the MD-81, but increased the fuel capacity with extra belly tanks and a greater gross take-off weight. Landing at Zürich Airport's runway 28, in August 1998, is McDonnell Douglas MD-83 HB-IKM c/n 49935 of Swiss holiday charter company Edelweiss Air. Today, this carrier operates both long-haul and short-haul services. This aircraft was sold on and withdrawn from use in the Netherland Antilles in 2017.

Pictured in October 1998 at its gate at Tucson International Airport, Arizona, is McDonnell Douglas MD-83 N878RA c/n 53184 of Reno Air, based at Nevada/Reno-Tahoe International Airport. The company had started services in July 1992 but were taken over by American Airlines in August 1999. This aircraft is now in service with an airline in Iran.

Since increasingly lengthy aircraft do not always fit the plans of some airlines, the McDonnell Douglas MD-87 was reduced in size by 28ft 9in (8.76m) and was able to carry 139 passengers. Landing at Manchester Airport, in September 1996, is McDonnell Douglas MD-87 SE-DHG c/n 49389 operated by Transwede Leisure. This carrier now operate as TUI fly Nordic. This aircraft was sold to a company in Argentina and was put into store in 2017.

McDonnell Douglas based the MD-88 on the size of the MD-82, but fitted it with a new cockpit featuring EFIS (Electronic Flight Information System) and FMS (Flight Management System). Landing at Miami International Airport, in October 1998, is McDonnell Douglas MD-88 N963DL c/n 49982 of Atlanta-based Delta Air Lines. This aircraft worked for the company all its operational life and was put into store in Blytheville, Arkansas, in March 2020.

The MD-90-30 was the size of the MD-88, but it was now fitted with two International Aero Engines' IAE V2528 turbofans with a power output of 25,000lb st. Pictured in October 1999 landing at Guangzhou, China, is McDonnell Douglas MD-90-30 B-2256 c/n 53582 of Shanghai-based China Eastern Airlines. This aircraft was sold on to Delta Air Lines in the United States and put into store in 2020 in Blytheville, Arkansas.

First flown in 1958, the Douglas DC-8 has outlasted its two main rivals, the Boeing 707 and the Convair 880. This is primarily because of its excellent design; a fuselage that could be extended and a programme of refitting modern, cleaner and fuel-efficient CFM-56s engines. These adaptions ensured that this model served many major cargo carriers well into the new millennium. Pictured in June 1990 at Willow Run Airport, Detroit, is Douglas DC-8-51F N804CK c/n 45689 operated by Connie Kalitta Services, an all-freight carrier specialising in parts delivery for the local motor industry. They were later renamed American International Airlines. This aircraft was broken up in Oscoda, Michigan.

Pictured at Hamilton International Airport, Ontario, whilst in store in June 1990, is Douglas DC-8-52 C-FNZE c/n 45985 of Edmonton, Alberta-based holiday charter operator, Points of Call Canada. They had suspended services in January of that year and this 170-seat aircraft was their total fleet. It was converted to a freighter in 1992 and, after six years of operations in Florida, it was broken up in Miami.

Lima-based AeroPeru (Empresa de Transporte Aéreo del Perú) operated a mixed fleet of passenger and cargo aircraft. Pictured in November 1992 at Barranquilla Airport, Colombia, is Douglas DC-8-54F N43UA c/n 45677. The extra titles belong to Sitra Cargo System who jointly operated the aircraft with them. The airline ceased operations in March 1999 and this aircraft was written off in a fatal crash at Guatemala City, Guatemala, Central America, in April 1995. It landed in light rain and overran the runway, causing the aircraft to go through the perimeter fence and down a slope towards a residential area.

The DC-8-61 series was stretched by 20ft (6.09m) forward of the wing and 16ft 8in (5.08m) aft. In a passenger role it could seat up to 259 people. However, by the 1990s, most were freighters. Lined up to take off at Miami International Airport, in April 1994, is Douglas DC-8-61F N27UA c/n 45942 of locally based Fine Air (an all-cargo carrier). In January 2001, they merged with Arrow Air. This aircraft was written off following a fatal crash at its base at Miami International Airport in August 1997. This occurred on take-off because of incorrectly loaded cargo, which affected the aircraft's centre of gravity.

The DC-8-62 series was designed for long-range operations and was stretched a further 3ft 4in (1.01m) both forward and aft of the wing. The wings themselves were extended and the aircraft had a greater fuel capacity. Pictured in March 1997 at Sharjah International Airport, UAE, is Douglas DC-8-62F LX-TLB c/n 45925 operated by Cargo Lion. Based in Luxemburg, they were an all-cargo carrier that ultimately suspended operations in April 2001 for financial reasons. This aircraft was withdrawn from service that year and broken up in Manston, Kent.

The -63 series of the DC-8 was an amalgam of the -61 and -62. It had the longer range of the -62, but the shorter fuselage of the -61. Lined up to depart from its base at Dublin Airport, in June 1994, is Douglas DC-8-63F EI-CGO c/n 45924 of Aer Turas Teoranta (Irish Cargo Airlines). They ceased operations in April 2003 and this aircraft was sold to a carrier in Africa and eventually broken up in 2013 in Lagos, Nigeria.

Formed in 1977, by former Douglas Aircraft Company staff, Cammacorp planned to re-engine the DC-8 with the SNECMA/GE CFM-56 turbofan. It was this power plant that gave the DC-8 many more years of economic service life. The thrust from this was 22,000lb st (the original -11 DC-8 had an output of 13,00lb st). The designations for the new variant were quite simple, since only the 'sixty series' were converted; the -61 became -71 and so on. The Federal Aviation Administration (FAA) certified the first -71 in April 1981 and the remaining two versions the following month. Delta Air Lines was the first airline to begin revenue passenger service on 24 April 1981. Pictured at Manchester Airport, in July 1993, is Douglas DC-8-71 EI-TLC c/n 45995 of Translift Airways, which are based in the west of Ireland at Shannon. This aircraft was passenger configured with 256 all economy seats. The carrier was renamed TransAer International Airlines and this aircraft was sold in the United States. After the sale, it was converted to a freighter in 1994 and in 2006 it was withdrawn and later broken up.

In a very smart livery, Douglas DC-8-71F CC-CAX c/n 45970 lines up to take off at Miami International Airport, in October 1998. Chilean airline Fast Air leased this aircraft to MAS Air Cargo of Mexico City. In 2016, Fast Air were rebranded as LATAM Cargo Mexico. This aircraft was withdrawn from use in 2004 in Manaus, Brazil, and stored, albeit in poor condition and without engines.

In the cargo area of Miami International Airport, in October 1998, is Douglas DC-8-71F CC-CDS c/n 45996 of LAN Chile Cargo. This aircraft was sold to an American carrier in 2000, stored in Roswell, New Mexico, in 2002 and later broken up.

Landing at Miami International Airport against a backdrop of rain filled clouds, in April 1994, is Douglas DC-8-71F CC-CAR c/n 45976 of Fast Air. They had been formed in 1974 and were merged into LADECO following their purchase by LAN Chile in 1998. This aircraft was sold to a company in Colombia and written off in a landing accident at Miami International Airport in February 2007. It landed on runway 09R and, following the deployment of the thrust reversers, the aircraft began to veer to the right. The landing gear had collapsed on one side and it was deemed to be beyond economic repair.

Pictured in March 1997 at Sharjah International Airport, UAE, is Douglas DC-8-73F N875SJ c/n 46063 of Southern Air Transport (SAT). An all-cargo airline, SAT had once been owned by the CIA. However, they sold their interest in 1973. In March 1999, its assets were sold to Southern Air who commenced operations in November of that year. This aircraft stayed with American operators and was sold on twice before it was stored in Roswell, New Mexico, in 2001 and later broken up. Today only a very small number of DC-8s can be found in service.

The Douglas DC-10 was first flown in August 1970. It was a wide-bodied, twin-aisled airliner, powered by three General Electric CF-6 turbofans with a thrust output of 39,300lb st. With an order for 25 and the same number of options, American Airlines were the launch customer. August 1971 saw the first revenue service with a flight from Los Angeles to Chicago. Pictured in November 1992 at Luis Muñoz Marín International Airport (SJA), San Juan, Puerto Rico, is McDonnell Douglas DC-10-10 N133AA c/n 47828 of American Airlines, today one of the largest carriers in the United States. This aircraft was sold to Hawaiian Airlines in 2001 and then converted to a freighter with FedEx in 2003. It became an MD-10F by bringing the cockpit to the same configuration as the later MD-11 aircraft. It was put into store in Victorville, California, in 2014.

Pictured in November 1992 arriving at Simón Bolívar International Airport, Caracas, is McDonnell Douglas DC-10-30 PH-DTB c/n 46551 of Dutch flag carrier KLM (Koninklijke Luchtvaart Maatschappij). The DC-10-30 was the long-range variant, which boasted upgraded CF-6-50 engines with an output of 48,000lb st and extra fuel tanks. Because of the extra weight, the -30 had a central undercarriage leg fitted. This aircraft served KLM for three more years before being sold in the United States; it was withdrawn in 2006 and later broken up.

Pictured at London Heathrow, in July 1993, is McDonnell Douglas DC-10-30 9G-ANA c/n 48286 of Ghana Airways. After incurring large debts they suspended all services in 2004. This aircraft was impounded and stored in Rome in 2003 and later it was moved to the United States to be broken up for spare parts.

Viasa (Venezolana Internacional de Aviación SA) were the flag carrier for Venezuela before they were closed by their own government following mounting financial losses. Seen in November 1992 at its base at Simón Bolívar International Airport, Caracas, is McDonnell Douglas DC-10-30 YV-138C c/n 46557 of Viasa. This aircraft was stored in Marana, Arizona, and later broken up.

Pictured landing at Athens International Airport, in June 1993, is McDonnell Douglas DC-10-30 F-ODLZ c/n 46869 operated by AOM (Air Outré Mer). The French company operated holiday flights and the interior is configured in a three-class system: 10 first, 40 business and 181 economy seats. In September 2001, the company was merged into Air Lib (previously known as Air Liberté) and both companies were based at Paris Orly Airport. It was here that this aircraft was stored and then broken up in 2008.

Landing at London Heathrow, in July 1997, is McDonnell Douglas DC-10-30 S2-ACO c/n 46993 of Biman Bangladesh Airlines, the national airline based at Dhaka. This aircraft was withdrawn and stored there in 2014.

They say it is hard to keep a good man down and, after his UK-based airline failed in the 1980s, Sir Freddie Laker founded two more. Firstly, he launched Laker Airways (Bahamas) in 1992 and, later, a sister airline called Laker Airways, Inc in 1996. The former, while registered in the United States, was based in the Grand Bahamas. The latter was based at Fort Lauderdale Hollywood International Airport, Florida. Seen landing at Manchester Airport in June 1996, is McDonnell Douglas DC-10-30 N833LA c/n 46937of Laker Airways, Inc. As a holiday charter, it was an all-economy configuration and could seat 353 passengers. Sadly, the company had to suspend operations in October 2004. This aircraft was later converted to a freighter and joined a company in Bolivia, where it still operates.

Wearing the livery of two companies at Miami International Airport, in October 1998, is McDonnell Douglas DC-10-30F XA-TDC c/n 46891. One livery is of TAESA (Transportes Aéreos Ejecutivos), who were based in Mexico City. The other is the colours of New Southways, a TAESA affiliate. New Southways were a cargo agent and bought space on the aircraft, hence the joint titles. TAESA was declared bankrupt in February 2000, and, in the same year, this aircraft was sold to a carrier in Peru where it is now in storage.

Based in Moi International Airport, Mombasa, ASA (African Safari Airways) flew passengers from major European cities to its base and then overland to the game reserves of Kenya. Pictured at Frankfurt Airport, in June 1999, is McDonnell Douglas DC-10-30 5Y-MBA c/n 46952. It was in a three-class configuration with 40 first, 86 business and 148 economy seats. The company suspended operations in March 2008 and this aircraft was withdrawn from use and broken up in Kemble, United Kingdom, in 2004.

Seen in evening sun at Phoenix Sky Harbor International Airport, in October 1998, is McDonnell Douglas DC-10-30F N322FE c/n 47908 of the United States' small parcel and package delivery giant, FedEx. They became one of the largest users of this type of aircraft, as well as of its follow-up, the MD-11. This aircraft was sold to a company in Brazil and later put into store in Sanford, Florida.

The DC-10-40 had a much heavier take-off weight and was powered by three Pratt & Whitney JT9D-59A turbofans, each with an output of 47,000lb st. Seen on the move at Miami International Airport, in October 1998, is McDonnell Douglas DC-10-40F N157DM c/n 46920 of Florida-based Challenge Air Cargo. They were owned by American parcel giant UPS and renamed Centurion Air Cargo in August 2001. This aircraft was sold on and withdrawn from use in Opa Locka, Florida in 2009.

Following on from the DC-10 came the MD-11. It was perhaps sad to see one of the greatest airliner prefixes dropped; the 'DC' (Douglas Commercial) dated back to 1933. However, the new parent company wanted their initials on any new aircraft that were produced. The MD-11 first flew in January 1990 and was an improvement from the DC-10. It was longer by 18ft 6in (5.6m) and the cockpit was now just for two pilots. It no longer required a flight engineer as it had state-of-the-art flight instrumentation. The most notable change was the 8ft 9in (2.7m) winglets on an extended wing. Power came from three General Electric CF-6 turbofans, with an output of 61,500lb st; the Pratt & Whitney PW4460 was also available to customers. Pictured at Bangkok, in November 1999, is McDonnell Douglas MD-11 HB-IWG c/n 48452 of Swissair Asia. Swissair Asia was a subsidiary of Swissair, designed to operate services to Taiwan without upsetting the Beijing government. Swissair ceased operations in March 2002; this aircraft was converted to a freighter in 2006 and today serves with UPS in the United States.

On push back from its gate at Frankfurt Airport, in June 1997, is McDonnell Douglas MD-11 N807DE c/n 48478 of Atlanta-based Delta Air Lines. One of the problems with the MD-11 was that it initially failed to live up to the flight range promised by the manufacturer. This resulted in many airlines disposing of their fleets early on and led to a new role as a cargo aircraft. This aircraft was converted to a freighter in 2008 for FedEx and was put into store in Victorville, California in 2019.

Pictured on its approach to London Heathrow, in July 1995, is McDonnell Douglas MD-11 PP-VOP c/n 48434 of Brazilian carrier VARIG (Viação Aérea Rio-Grandense). Like many South African airlines, VARIG had a long career extending throughout the 20th century; they were established in 1927. This aircraft was sold on in 2000 and converted to a freighter. Whilst operated by an American cargo company, the aircraft was written off in October 2012 in a landing accident in São Paulo, Brazil. On touch down, the left-side main gear collapsed and caused damage beyond economic repair. It is worth noting that, three years earlier, whilst under ownership from the same carrier, the aircraft landed in Uruguay and the right-hand main gear was bent sideways. In that case, however, the damage was deemed repairable.

About to land at Frankfurt Airport, in June 1997, is McDonnell Douglas MD-11 JA8583 c/n 48574 of Japan Airlines, one of the nation's two major carriers. This aircraft was sold on and converted to a freighter in 2003. It currently serves with UPS in the United States.

Under tow at Amsterdam Airport Schiphol, in August 1997, is McDonnell Douglas MD-11 B-150 c/n 48468 of Mandarin Airlines of Taiwan. Based in Chiang Kai Shek International Airport, this carrier continues to operate, primarily flying domestically and regional international services whilst their parent company, China Airlines, fly the long-haul. In many cases, despite being painted in Mandarin Airlines' livery, it could be also found to be operating China Airlines flights. This aircraft was written off at Hong Kong International Airport in August 1999 during a landing in bad weather. The aircraft broke apart and caught fire; remarkably, there were only three deaths among the 315 passengers and crew on board.

Arriving at its gate at Bangkok, in November 1999, is McDonnell Douglas MD-11 HS-TMF c/n 48418 of national airline Thai Airways International (Thai). This aircraft left the fleet in 2007 when it was converted to a freighter and currently serves with UPS in the United States. Whilst with Thai, this aircraft operated a passenger service with a three-class layout with 10 first, 42 business and 233 economy seats.

On the move at Amsterdam Airport Schiphol, in August 1997, is McDonnell Douglas MD-11 N103EV c/n 48415 of Taiwan-based carrier, Eva Air. The company continues to operate both passenger and cargo services across the world and to many cities in mainland China. This aircraft was sold on and converted to a freighter in 2004 and is currently with a company in the United States.

Lined up to take off at Miami International Airport, in October 1998, is McDonnell Douglas MD-11CF N276WA c/n 48632 operated by STAF (Servicios de Transportes Aéreos Fueguinos), based in Buenos Aires. The company would lease aircraft as required and they ceased operations in 2005. This aircraft was sold to FedEx in October 2012 for spare parts, stored in Victorville, California, and then parted out.

The Lockheed TriStar was the second twin-aisled, wide-bodied, three-engined airliner chasing to be in the order books of the world's carriers. However, it had a rocky start as the selected power plant for it was the Rolls-Royce RB-211. There were significant delays that, coupled with development costs, brought the company bankruptcy. Eventually, the company was nationalised by the then-Conservative government in London in 1971. The prototype first flew in November 1970. Pictured at Manchester Airport, in May 1996, is Lockheed L-1011 TriStar 1 N305GB c/n 1127 of Miami-based Rich International Airways. They flew a mix of passenger and cargo configured aircraft, this one being for passengers with 345 economy seats. The company ceased operations the following year and this aircraft went into store in Roswell, New Mexico, and was broken up. The registration was cancelled in 2004.

On pushback from its gate at Terminal One at Manchester Airport, in June 1996, is Lockheed L-1011 TriStar 1 TF-ABE c/n 1022 of Air Atlanta Iceland. This Reykjavik-based company were operating a holiday charter flight, as they continue to do. It had a two-class interior with 49 business and 250 economy seats. It was the only aircraft in their fleet with business class seats. This aircraft was stored in Marana, Arizona, and broken up in 2004.

The TriStar 50 had a stronger structure and a higher gross take-off weight. Landing in April 1994 at Miami International Airport, with a backdrop of rain-filled clouds, is Lockheed L-1011 TriStar 50 OB-1545 c/n 1075 of Peru-based Faucett (Compãnia de Aviación Faucett). It was one of the oldest South American airlines and was founded in 1928 by American Elmer Faucett. They ceased operations in 1997 and this aircraft was broken up in Miami that year. It had been configured in a three-class layout.

Initially designed as a medium-range airliner, the TriStar 100 had two extra fuel tanks fitted in the centre section to extend the range. Seen at Manchester Airport, in March 1995, is Lockheed L-1011 TriStar 100 G-BBAJ c/n 1106 of Caledonian Airways. The Gatwick-based holiday charter operator merged with Flying Colours and other carriers to form JMC Air in September 1999. As a low-cost holiday carrier, Caledonian Airways configured all of their aircraft to an all-economy layout with 393 seats. The fleet all donned names of Scottish lochs, with this G-BBAJ being called *Loch Rannoch*. It was stored and broken up in 2004 in Al Hoceima, Morocco.

Air Transat are a Canadian charter operator based in Montreal, who continue to operate today. Seen landing at Manchester Airport, in August 1995, is Lockheed L-1011 TriStar 150 C-FTNH c/n 1049. The -150 was a variant that had an even heavier gross take-off weight than the -50; this weight was increased by 20,000lb (9072kg) to bring it to 470,000lb (213,188kg). As holiday charter, this aircraft had seats for 340 economy passengers. It was withdrawn and broken up at the company base in 2002.

Pictured on approach to Miami International Airport, in October 1998, is Lockheed L-1011 TriStar 200F N307GB c/n 1131 of Arrow Air, a locally based all-cargo carrier. In January 2001, this carrier was merged into Fine Air. The -200's hot and high performance was improved and a newer Rolls-Royce RB211-524 power plant was installed, which had an output of 50,000lb st. This aircraft was put into store in 2004 and broken up two years later in Roswell, New Mexico.

The TriStar -500 was the long-range variant, with extra fuel tanks in the centre section. It was shortened by 13ft 6in (4.11m) in the fuselage and the wing span was increased by 9ft (2.74m). Pictured landing at Miami International Airport, in April 1994, is Lockheed L-1011 TriStar 500 D-AERL c/n 1196 of LTU (Luft Transport Unternehmen). They were a Düsseldorf-based holiday charter carrier and they merged with Air Berlin in 2009. This 288-seater was withdrawn and stored in Roswell, New Mexico, and broken up in 2002.

Seen in September 1995 at Sheremetyevo International Airport, Moscow, is Lockheed L-1011 TriStar 500 CS-TEC c/n 1241 of TAAG Angola Airlines (Linhase Aéreas de Angola). It was, and continues to be, the national airline. It was the largest aircraft in their fleet and on lease from TAP Air Portugal, hence the registration. This aircraft was put into store at Victorville Airport, California, and has been acquired by the TriStar History and Preservation Group, who plan to fly it to Kansas City where it will be preserved in Trans World Airlines' (TWA) colours. Despite being one of the largest users of the L-1011, TWA did not fly the short-body -500 version.

Heading for its gate at Amsterdam Airport Schiphol, in August 1997, is Lockheed L-1011 TriStar 500 JY-AGD c/n 1229 in the attractive livery of Jordan's flag carrier, Royal Jordanian. This aircraft was withdrawn and put into store in El Alamein, Egypt.

Pictured on approach to London Heathrow, in September 1993, is Lockheed L-1011 TriStar 500 9Y-TGN c/n 1191 of BWIA (British West Indies Airways of Trinidad and Tobago). The carrier ceased operations at the end of 2006. This aircraft was withdrawn and stored in Trinidad and, in December 2003, was preserved and put on display at the Chaguaramas Military Museum.

Launched by British Aerospace in July 1978, the BAe 146 was the first commercial airliner from that company. However, it did have its origins in several de Havilland designs, going back as far as 1959. The first flight was in September 1981 and it was certified in May the following year. The chosen power plants were four Lycoming (later Allied Signal) ALF 502 turbofans and this led to it being one of the quietest airliners flying. This was important in selling the aircraft to companies who operated in areas with strict noise regulations, such as Southern California, and airports like Orange County. The first variant, the -100, had the shortest fuselage and, when upgraded with more powerful engines and a modern flight deck, were designated as RJ-70 (Regional Jet). It also used the Avro name, given by one of the companies that had formed BAe. Pictured at Frankfurt Airport, in June 1997, is Avro RJ-70A YL-BAK c/n E1223 of Air Baltic, the current flag carrier of Latvia. This aircraft was sold on and then later stored.

The -200 version of the BAe 146 had a fuselage extension of 7ft 10in (2.38m) and first flew in August 1982. It could seat over 100 passengers at full capacity and it had increased fuel capacity. Seen at London Gatwick, in August 1993, is BAe 146-200 I-FLRW c/n E2178 of Meridiana, an Italian regional operator. In 2018, they were renamed Air Italy. This aircraft served with many operators and was last reported as in store in Yaoundé, Cameroon in 2015.

The -300 version of the 146 was the longest and had been stretched 8ft 1in (2.46m) forward and 7ft 8in (2.33m) aft of the wing. The prototype first flew in May 1987. Seen landing at London Heathrow, in July 1997, is Avro RJ-100 HB-IXS c/n E3280 of Switzerland-based Crossair. They called the type the 'Jumbolino'. The company had been a regional carrier but, when Swissair collapsed, they took on many of their routes and aircraft. They now simply use the name Swiss. This aircraft was sold on and is currently in store with a company in Chile.

July 1960 saw the formation of the British Aircraft Corporation (BAC). It was an amalgamation of Vickers-Armstrong, Bristol Aeroplane Company and English Electric Aviation, which, together, then took over Hunting Aircraft. The first airliner from the new group was the BAC 1-11; a jet airliner with twin rear-mounted Rolls-Royce Spey turbofans. The first flight was in August 1963 and, by that time, it had accumulated a good order book, including purchases from several large American airlines. The -500 series was stretched by 13ft 6in (4.11m) and entered service in the summer of 1969. Pictured on approach to London Gatwick, in August 1997, is BAC 1-11 510ED G-AVMW c/n 150 of AB Airlines. Named after the city in which they were based, they started in 1993 as Air Bristol and took the current shorter name in 1996. Services were suspended in 1999 and this aircraft was broken up in Bournemouth, UK, in 2002.

Seen at Athens International Airport, in June 1993, is ROMBAC 1-11 516RC YR-BRC c/n 403 of Romanian national airline Tarom (Transporturile Aeriene Romane). This aircraft was one of the aircraft built under licence by IRMA (Intreprinderea de Reparatii Material Aeronautic). The agreement between BAC and IRMA, in June 1979, was to continue to build the 1-11 in Romania when the UK-based line closed in 1981. The first one flew in September 1982. However, owing to a disastrous lack of sales, only nine aircraft had been built by the end of 1989. This was a time of turmoil in Eastern Europe and production coincided with a time of mass political upheaval as the Romanian president was put on trial and shot. Various rescue plans for the company came to nothing and the 1-11 line was finally closed. This aircraft was sold on and put into store in 2009. It was broken up in Ras Al Khaimah, UAE, the following year.

The Sud Aviation Caravelle was a ground-breaking, western twin-jet airliner. It was the first of its kind; the prototype first flew in 1955 and the aircraft entered service in April 1959 with SAS (Scandinavian Airline System). They surpassed Air France by one week because SAS had used one of the prototypes to train their pilots. The first service was from Copenhagen to Beirut. The original power plants were Rolls-Royce Avons but later variants had Pratt & Whitney JT8D-9s with an output of 14,500lb st. By the 1990s, the Caravelle was a rare sight in the world. However, pictured at Bogotá, in November 1992, is Sud Aviation SE-210 Caravelle 10B-3 HK-3756X c/n 259 of Líneas Aéreas Suramericanas (LASA), who are based locally. They were an all-cargo carrier and only a handful of Caravelles ever operated in this capacity. This aircraft was withdrawn from use and broken up in 2002.

Pictured landing on its regular daily service from Damascus to Athens, in June 1993, is Sud Aviation SE-210 Caravelle 10B-3 YK-AFD c/n 186 of Syrianair – Syrian Arab Airlines, the national carrier. By this time, this carrier had just two Caravelles in their fleet. They were configured with seven first class and 63 economy seats. Owing to the current civil war, the carrier is banned from services to the European Union. This aircraft was withdrawn, at base, in 1995.

It is quite uncommon for an airliner to be developed from a business jet but the Canadair CRJ (Regional Jet) was derived from the Challenger. It had a stretched fuselage that could accommodate 50 passengers, a T-tail, an enlarged wing with winglets and a pair of rear mounted General Electric CF-34 turbofans. The prototype first flew in May 1991 and the launch customer, Lufthansa CityLine, put them into revenue service the following year. Seen at Frankfurt Airport, in June 1997, is Canadair CRJ-100LR OE-LRG c/n 7063 of Vienna-based Lauda Air. The company had been founded by Formula 1 world champion, and qualified commercial pilot, Nikki Lauda in 1985 as an air taxi and charter company. They were taken over by Austrian Airlines at the end of 2000 and this aircraft was sold on and in 2006 broken up in Montreal, Canada.

Pictured in October 1998 at Phoenix Sky Harbor International Airport, Arizona, is Canadair CRJ-200LR N27173 c/n 7173 of locally based carrier, Mesa Airlines. They flew both as themselves and also as a service company for large airlines operating their commuter flights. These larger airlines included US Airways Express and America West Express and the aircraft often wore that company's livery. The CJR-200 variant had up rated engines and extended range. This aircraft was sold in 2013 to Amaszonas of La Paz, Bolivia.

Dutch aircraft manufacturer Fokker followed up their best-selling turboprop, the F.27 Friendship, with a jet replacement named the F.28 Fellowship. Powered by a pair of Rolls-Royce Spey turbofans, it first flew in May 1967 and could hold up to 65 passengers. Pictured at Düsseldorf International Airport, in September 1998, is Fokker F.28 Fellowship 4000 YU-AOH c/n 11184 of Podgorica-based Montenegro Airlines. They had started operations the previous year and were closed down at the end of 2020. The -4000 had a longer fuselage, a wider wingspan and improved engines. This aircraft was configured to seat 75 passengers. It was sold to an airline in Myanmar and withdrawn from use in 2012.

Fokker brought the F.28 up to date with two new models. These were the Fokker 100 and the Fokker 70, the latter of which was shorter by 15ft 2in (4.62m). These two were now powered by much more fuel efficient and quieter Rolls-Royce Tay 620 turbofans with an output of 13,850lb st. In the cockpit was new electronic flight instrumentation. The prototype Fokker 70 flew in April 1993. Pictured at Frankfurt Airport, in June 1999, is Fokker 70 PH-WXA c/n 11570 of KLM Cityhopper. This carrier is a subsidiary of KLM and they fly regional services around Europe. This aircraft operated in a one-class, 80 seat layout. It was sold on and is currently with an airline in Brazil.

When it was introduced in 1967, the Beechcraft Model 99 was the largest aircraft from the well-established company known for their small private types. The market for the new aircraft was the air taxi and commuter airlines. Power came from a pair of Pratt & Whitney Canada PT-6 turboprops with an output of 550shp. Pictured in June 1990 on its way back to the company base at Sioux Lookout Airport, Ontario, from a charter to Pickle Lake Airport, Ontario, is Beech 99 Airliner C-GFQC c/n U-120 of Bearskin Air. It was fitted out for 14 passengers. The company is still in operation and flies from a mix of remote settlements in Ontario, and surrounding provinces, to major cities. This aircraft was withdrawn from use in 2016.

The Beechcraft 1900 Airliner was powered by a pair of Pratt & Whitney Canada PT-6A -65Bs with an output of 1,100shp. It first flew in September 1982 and could seat 19 in pressurised comfort. Pictured in June 1990 awaiting its next set of passengers at Sioux Lookout Airport, Ontario, is Beech 1900C-1 Airliner C-GFAD c/n UC-83 in the colours of Canadian Frontier. It was operated by Ontario Express, who flew commuter services in the far north of the country for the parent carrier, Canadian Airlines International. In 2001, the parent carrier was merged into Air Canada. This aircraft is currently in operation in Alaska.

There is a vast difference between the Beechcraft 1900C and the 1900D. The 1900D had the cabin volume expanded by 28.5 per cent, with winglets fitted and ventral strakes to increase the directional stability. The Pratt & Whitney Canada PT-6-67D turboprops were rated at 1,279shp. The prototype flew for the first time in March 1990 and it was certified a year later. Seen at Phoenix Sky Harbor Airport in October 1998, is Beech 1900D Airliner N93ZV c/n UE-93 in the colours of America West Express. It was operated for them by Mesa Airlines, which were one of the largest operators of the type. Despite the extra size of the cabin it still only had seats for 19 passengers. This aircraft is still in use with an operator in Colombia.

One of the most versatile aircraft flying today is the Britten-Norman Islander. It was designed to be operated anywhere in the world. It had a fixed undercarriage and simple systems and was powered by a pair of Lycoming piston engines of 260hp. The prototype first flew in June 1965 and could seat up to ten passengers. Over the years, the company has been bought and sold several times. Pictured in November 1992 at its base in La Vanguardia Airport, Villavicencio, Colombia, is Britten-Norman BN-2 Islander HK-2822 c/n 2109 operated by ARO Colombia (Aérovias Regionles del Oriente). This company still operates, and the aircraft now serves with Aeroupia at the same location.

A stretched version of the Britten-Norman Islander was first flown in September 1970 and featured a third Lycoming piston engine mounted on the fin. The new aircraft could carry up to 17 passengers. Pictured in November 1992 at Simón Bolívar International Airport, Caracas, Venezuela, is Britten-Norman BN-2A Mk.111-2 Trislander YV-488C c/n 1012 of CAVE (Compania Aérea de Viajes Expressos), a local commuter operator. They suspended services the following year. This aircraft was sold on and damaged beyond economic repair in North Perry, Florida, during a hurricane in February 1998.

De Havilland Aircraft of Canada has established a reputation for building excellent aircraft with a short take-off and landing (STOL) performance. One such was the DHC-7 Dash Seven, a high-wing, four-engine commuter seating up to 50 people. Power was from Pratt & Whitney Canada PT-6A-50 turboprops of 1,035shp. It first flew in March 1975. Its performance and noise level was such that, in the early years of London City Airport, it was the only type to be able to fly services. Pictured in November 1992 at its hangar at El Dorado International Airport, Bogotá, is de Havilland Canada DHC-7 Dash Seven 102 HK-3112G c/n 88 owned by Helicol. This local company serviced the country's oil and gas industry with both helicopters and fixed-wing aircraft. It was being operated for Intercor, a Colombian natural resource company. This aircraft was sold on and joined the US Army, where it still serves.

Following on from the Dash Seven came the DHC-8 Dash Eight. It was a twin turboprop and the fuselage was cleverly designed to be extended over different models, as demand for more seats grew. Pictured landing at Miami International Airport, in October 1998, is de Havilland Canada DHC-8 Dash Eight 202 N987HA c/n 425 in the livery of US Air Express. It is another example of a carrier – in this instance, Piedmont Airlines – operating franchise services for a larger company (US Air Express) in their colour scheme and using their flight numbers. US Air Express are now part of American Airlines and this aircraft joined the US Air Force in 2018, where it still serves.

One of the most elusive goals for aircraft manufactures was that of the so-called Dakota replacement. Some of the aircraft built in this pursuit had long lives, while others had much shorter. The Dakota, however, is still in service in some parts of the world today. The British company Handley Page, one of the oldest aircraft builders in the world, attempted a replacement with the Herald. In its first iteration, it was powered by four Alvis Leonides piston engines and flew in August 1955. The company decided to replace the engine design with a pair of Rolls-Royce Dart turboprops; this model flew in March 1958 and was known as the Dart Herald. Pictured at Liverpool Airport, in October 1996, is a Handley Page HPR-7 Dart Herald 214 G-CEAS c/n 186 of Channel Express. By 1996, few Heralds were still to be found in service and those that were had been configured for cargo. This aircraft was withdrawn from use and broken up in November 1997. Channel Express was an all-cargo airline based in Bournemouth and, in 2006, they rebranded themselves as Jet2 and moved into holiday flights.

With the success of the Viscount Vickers, the manufacturer Vickers-Armstrong looked to build a larger capacity aircraft that was still powered by four turboprops. The new prototype, the Vickers Vanguard, first flew in January 1959. Unfortunately, despite their best efforts to sell the aircraft, only 43 were built for just two airlines, British European Airways and Trans-Canada Air Lines. A small number were later converted to freighters with a large forward door and a stronger floor. Those converted were called Merchantman. Pictured at East Midlands Airport, in July 1991, is Vickers 953C Vanguard/Merchantman G-APET c/n 722 of Air Bridge. They were an all-cargo carrier and, in 1992, were rebranded as Hunting Cargo Airlines. This aircraft was withdrawn at East Midlands Airport and broken up in May 1997.

Production of the Lockheed C-130 Hercules began in 1954 and, albeit with many updates, is still going strong. For over 50 years, it has been the transportation backbone of many of the world's air forces. A civil version has also been sold to the cargo divisions of airlines. Pictured on the runway after landing at Frankfurt Airport, in June 1999, is Lockheed L382G Hercules 7T-VHG c/n 51C-4880. It is operated by Air Algérie, the national airline. This aircraft was written off in Italy in August 2006, due to loss of control in bad weather.

First flown in 1957, the Lockheed Electra was powered by four Allison 501 turboprops with an output of 3750shp. When it entered service with Eastern Air Lines in January 1959, the ticket buying public had become accustomed to the appearance of jets and, despite them being state-of-the-art, did not want to see anything with propellers. Therefore, this aircraft had a relatively short life with the major carriers. However, it went on to have a long life with smaller airlines and still serves as a cargo carrier to this day. Pictured in June 1990 on the ramp at Willow Run Airport, Michigan, with all four engines turning is Lockheed L-188PF Electra N341HA c/n 1035 of Zantop International Airlines. This local airline was an all-freight carrier specialising in the local motor industry. The company put their fleet up for sale in March 1997 and drastically scaled back their operations. Their last flight was in September 2005. This aircraft was put into store in Willow Run Airport in 1997 and finally broken up in 2006.

The Royal Canadian Air Force (RCAF) had a need for a transport aircraft. Canadair attempted to fulfil this need by taking inspiration from Bristol Aeroplane Company's Britannia, but with the addition of Rolls-Royce Tyne turboprops. Their product, the CC-106 Yukon, had large cargo doors on the front and rear of the left-hand side of the fuselage. Once all 12 of the aircraft for the RCAF had been built, Canadair were keen to sell the new aircraft as a specialist cargo aircraft to a wider market. They developed a swing tail system in which the whole unit was on a hinge and could open for the ease of loading long objects. This aircraft was the CL-44D4; 27 were built and first flew in November 1960. Pictured in November 1992 arriving at Las Américas International Airport, Santo Domingo, Dominican Republic, is Canadair CL-44D4-2 N106BB c/n 37 of Greensboro, North Carolina-based all-freight carrier, Tradewinds International Airlines. The company experienced severe financial trouble in July 2008 for the third time and in December of that year they were bought by Sky Lease Cargo from Florida. This aircraft was sold on and, in April 2000, whilst being operated by the air force of the Democratic Republic of Congo, the aircraft was destroyed. The damage was caused by a major fire and the subsequent explosion of ammunition in a warehouse at Kinshasa Airport in the Democratic Republic of Congo.

The first, and only, post-war Japanese-manufactured aircraft to enter service was the NAMC Nihon Aircraft Manufacturing Company's YS-11. It first flew in 1962 and was another attempt at creating the so-called DC-3 replacement. Like all the others it was powered by a pair of Rolls-Royce Darts. It sold moderately well and was operated worldwide. Pictured in June 1990 on the ramp at Willow Run Airport, Detroit, Michigan, is NAMC YS-11A -310 N125MP c/n 2070 of Mid Pacific Cargo. The company had moved from their original home of Hawaii – hence the name – to Indiana and operations closed in 1995. This aircraft was sold on several times and, at one point, impounded by the authorities in Colombia for alleged drug running. It was sold on once more and taken to Mexico, where it was put in store but in poor condition.

Another short take-off and landing aircraft from de Havilland Aircraft of Canada was the Twin Otter. The first one flew in May 1965 and was powered by a pair of Pratt & Whitney Canada PT-6A turboprops. Since its launch, the aircraft has been sold to both commuter airlines – as it can seat up to 19 passengers – as well as to many air forces. Pictured in November 1992 at its base at El Dorado International Airport, Bogotá, is de Havilland Canada DHC-6 Twin Otter 300 HK-2970X c/n 781 of Helicol. The -300 series had the longer nose of the -200 and the PT-6 engines were rated at 652shp. This aircraft currently operates in the Maldives, where it is now equipped with floats to transport tourists to their atoll hotels.

Short Brothers (commonly referred to as Shorts) of Belfast developed the SD330, a small turboprop transport aircraft, from the box-like Short SC.7 Skyvan. It was larger and had a retractable undercarriage and PT-6A turboprops. It first flew in August 1974 and could carry 30 passengers. Pictured at Athens International Airport, in June 1993, is Short SD330-100 SX-BGC c/n SH3065 of Olympic Aviation. This division of Olympic Airways operated the commuter services around the Greek Islands. This aircraft was withdrawn in Athens in 1994 and broken up three years later.

Following the Short Brothers SD330 came the SD360. It was longer, had a single fin, PT-6A engines with an output of 1327shp and could carry 36 passengers. It first flew in June 1981. Pictured at Liverpool Airport, in June 1994, is Short SD360-100 G-OLAH c/n SH3604 of Newcastle-based Gill Air. The company ceased operations in September 2001. In this same year, this aircraft was sold on and was broken up.

The most successful of the two British-built DC-3 replacements was the Avro (later Hawker Siddeley) 748. It was the last aircraft to be produced by Avro before becoming absorbed into Hawker Siddeley (and later British Aerospace). First flying in June 1960, it was, like all the others, powered by a trusty pair of Rolls-Royce Darts. It sold worldwide and was built under licence in India by Hindustan Aeronautics. By the 1990s, many of those in service were freighters. Pictured in June 1990 at its base at Pickle Lake Airport, Ontario, is Hawker Siddeley HS-748-244 Srs.2 C-GLTC c/n 1656 of Kelner Airways. They flew a mixed fleet of passenger and cargo aircraft around the north of the province. In January 1993, they were renamed Wasaya Airways. This aircraft is still in service with the company.

Pictured at Liverpool Airport, in July 1997, is Hawker Siddeley HS-748-378 Srs.2B G-OJEM c/n 1791 of Liverpool-based Emerald Airways. The company flew mainly freight but did, on occasion, operate passenger services to the Isle of Man. They were closed down in 2006. This aircraft was equipped to seat 44 people and was damaged beyond economic repair in March 1998 at Stansted. It suffered an engine fire on take-off and, when it landed, ran off the end of the runway with a collapsed nose wheel.

Following on from the HS 748, Hawker Siddeley (now known as British Aerospace) developed a stretched, re-engined version with modern cockpit instruments. This was known as the ATP or 'Advanced Turboprop'. It first flew in August 1986 and powered by a pair of Pratt & Whitney PW124A engines with an output of 2653shp. It had been stretched by 16ft 6in (5.03m), the vertical fin had been modified and the wingspan increased. Pictured at Manchester Airport, in April 1991, is BAe ATP G-OLCD c/n 2018 of Glasgow-based Loganair. The company operate services around the UK and also serve the small Scottish islands. This aircraft was converted to a cargo carrier and is now with an airline in Sweden.

Following the demise of Handley Page's HP.137 Jetstream, British Aerospace (BAe) developed it into the Jetstream 31. Production was based in Prestwick in Scotland and the aircraft first flew in March 1980, with certification in June 1982. The chosen power plant was a pair of Garrett TPE331 turboprops of 1020shp. The aircraft had a passenger capacity of 19. Pictured in June 1998 at Kuopio Airport, Finland, is BAe 3201 Jetstream 32 OH-JAB c/n 835 of Air Botnia. Based in Helsinki, the airline was later renamed Blue1. This aircraft was sold on in the United States and withdrawn in 2013.

Following the development of BAe's Jetstream 31 came the Jetstream 41. It was longer by 8ft 3in (2.51m) ahead and 7ft 9in (2.36m) aft of the wing; power came from Garrett TPE331 turboprops with 1500shp. The aircraft could seat 29 passengers, and first flight was in September 1991. Seen at Newcastle International Airport, in September 1998, is BAe 4100 Jetstream 41 G-MSKJ c/n 41034 of Maersk Air. They were based in Birmingham and flew franchise services for British Airways with aircraft in BA livery. This carries one of the Utopia or 'World Image' schemes; this particular design was created by Martha Masanabo of the Ndebele people of South Africa. Maersk Air became Duo Airways in 2003 following a management buyout. This airframe is currently with a carrier in Zambia.

The most successful airliner from any post-war British company must be Vickers-Armstrongs' aircraft, the Viscount. It first flew in July 1948 and an enlarged production aircraft flew in August 1950. It sold worldwide, with especially large numbers going to America. Pictured landing at Manchester Airport, in April 1991, is Vickers Viscount 802 G-AOHM c/n 162 of British United Air Ferries (BUAF). Based at Southend, they flew a mix of passenger and cargo aircraft. This aircraft was configured with 74 economy class seats. In April 1993, BUAF were renamed British World Airlines. This aircraft was sold and came to grief in N'Djamena, Chad, in July 2001. The pilot aborted take-off and the aircraft ran off the side of the runway with damage to two of the Rolls-Royce Darts. While seemingly damaged beyond economic repair, attempts were made to repair it. However, when the repairs were nearly complete, a soldier, who was asleep under the wing, accidentally discharged his gun and punctured one of the fuel tanks. The aircraft was later reported to have been broken up.

The best-seller of all the so-called DC-3 replacements was the Fokker F.27 Friendship. Like all the others, it had Rolls-Royce Darts. The prototype took to the skies in November 1955 and launch customer, Aer Lingus, received their first one in March 1958. Pictured landing at London Heathrow, in October 1993, is Fokker F.27 Friendship 200 G-BHMY c/n 10196 of Air UK. The -200 variant had increased fuel capacity, improved engines. It could seat up to 48 passengers, although this specific aircraft is configured for 44. Air UK was taken over by KLM in 1997 and renamed KLM uk. This aircraft has been preserved at the Norwich Aviation Museum following the end of its service life in 1998.

Fokker's F.27 Friendship was licence built in the United States by Fairchild Aircraft in Hagerstown, Maryland. The aircraft built under licence exhibited a number of minor differences to the original Dutch-built ones; these included heavier skinning and improved electrical and air conditioning systems. Pictured at Kendall-Tamiami Executive Airport, in October 1998, is Fairchild F-27A Friendship YN-CER c/n 30 of LADECO (Línea Aérea de Cobra). This carrier was based in Nicaragua and suspended operation in 1999. This aircraft was withdrawn, stored and then broken up.

While Fokker's F.27 Friendship was being built under licence by Fairchild Aircraft in the United States, the latter extended the Friendship fuselage by 6ft 6in (1.98m). This increased the seating capacity from 48 passengers to 56. Pictured in September 1997 on the ramp at Mariscal Sucre International Airport, Quito, is Fairchild FH-227B HC-BXC c/n 533 of Austro Aéreo. The carrier flew scheduled services from its base at Cuenca. They were declared bankrupt in 2003 and ceased operations. This aircraft went into store at their base.

To bring the F.27 Friendship up to date, the original manufacturer brought out the Fokker 50. It had new power plants in the form of 2160shp Pratt & Whitney PW124 turboprops. It also had a longer nose, new cockpit instrumentation and could seat up to 58 passengers. It first flew in December 1985. Pictured landing at its base at Dublin Airport, in June 1994, is Fokker 50 EI-FKD c/n 20181 of Irish national airline Aer Lingus. This aircraft has been sold on and is now in store.

Jointly developed by Fairchild Aircraft and Swearingen Aircraft, the Metroliner was a 19-seat commuter aircraft with a pair of Garrett TPE331 turboprops. Alongside the passenger version of the aircraft, a dedicated freighter was also built. Pictured at Winnipeg International Airport, in June 1990, is Swearingen SA227AT Expediter N566UP c/n AT-566. It is owned by Merlin Express of San Antonio, Texas, who operate the aircraft for, and in the full colours of, UPS. This aircraft was sold on, but retains the same job with another US carrier.

The manufacturer ATR (Avions de Transport Régional) was set up by French company Aérospatiale and Italy's Aeritalia in 1981. The aim was to build a twin turboprop for regional services; the outcome was the ATR 42, which first flew in August 1984. The number 42 reflected the aircraft's seating capacity. It was a high-wing, T-tail commuter aircraft, powered by a pair of 1800shp Pratt & Whitney Canada PW120 engines. Pictured in November 1992 on the ramp at Olaya Herrera Airport, Medellin, Colombia, is ATR 42-320 HK-3684X c/n 284 of ACES (Aerolineas Centrales de Colombia). They flew both domestic and regional international services from their Medellin base. August 2003 saw the end of operations. This aircraft was sold on to several South American operators and it went into store in 2014. Note the policeman and sniffer dog by the nose of the aircraft; they are looking for one of the best-known exports from the town.

Following on from the ATR 42, Avions de Transport Régional developed the ATR 72 in October 1988. It was longer by 14ft 9in (4.49m) and the wingspan was wider by 8ft 1in (2.45m). The -72 reflected the aircraft's intended seating capacity. However, each operator would fix their own seat pitch. The power plants were Pratt & Whitney Canada PW 124Bs with an output of 2160shp. Pictured landing at Athens Airport, in June 1993, is ATR 72-202 SX-BIF c/n 241 of Olympic Aviation. After being sold on, this aircraft now operates in Canada.

Formed in 1969, Embraer (Empresa Brasileira de Aeronáutica SA) has grown in size to be one of the major aircraft manufacturers of commuter-size turboprop and smaller jet airliners. Their first was the EMB 110 Bandeirante, which first took to the air in August 1972. Sales were just short of 500 and many of them went to operators in the United States. Pictured in November 1992 at La Vanguardia Airport, Villavicencio, is Embraer EMB-110P Bandeirante HK-2741 c/n 110380 of Bogotá-based AIRES (Aerovias de Integracíon Regional SA). At the end of 2011, AIRES were rebranded LAN Colombia. This aircraft was withdrawn at base in 2001.

Following on from the EMB 110 Bandeirante, Embraer produced the EMB 120 Brasilia; first flying in July 1983. It was powered by two Pratt & Whitney PW115 turboprops of 1500shp and could seat up to 30 passengers. Pictured in June 1990 at Hamilton International Airport, Ontario, is Embraer EMB-120RT Brasilia C-GDOE c/n 120178 of Ontario Express. It is in the colours of Canadian Partner and operates services for Canadian Airlines International using their flight numbers. This aircraft was sold on several times and broken up for spare parts in 2005.

First flying in August 1995, the EMB-145 was Embraer's first regional jet. They based the fuselage upon their EMB 120 Brasilia, with some adjustments; it was 30ft 2in (9.19m) longer; it could seat 50 passengers; it had a new swept wing; and power was from a pair of rear mounted Allison AE3007A turbofans with an output of 7,040lb st. Seen at Zürich Airport, in August 1998, is Embraer EMB-145EU G-EMBB c/n 145021 of British Regional Airlines. The company fly services as a franchise using British Airways fight numbers and their aircraft in BA colours. They were the first operators of the aircraft in the UK. In March 2001, BA officially purchased the company and it was merged with Brymon Airways to form BA Citi Express. This aircraft has one of BA's 'World Image' tails; it is Sterntaler (also known as Bauhaus) by the German artist Antje Bruggermann. This aircraft was sold on and stored in Kingman, Arizona, in 2016.

Swedish manufacturer SAAB is well known for their production of advanced military aircraft. In fact, it was not until the 1980s that they returned to manufacturing civil aircraft, after a gap of 30 years. Their new aircraft, the SAAB 340, was designed for the commuter market and could seat up to 35 people. It was a twin-turboprop powered by General Electric's GE CT7s with an output of 1630shp. The prototype first flew in January 1983. Pictured on the move at Helsinki Airport, in June 1998, is SAAB 340A OH-FAD c/n 340A-135 in the colours of Finnaviation. The company had been absorbed into Finnair the previous year, but this aircraft had not yet been repainted. It was sold on and is now in service in New Zealand.

First flying in March 1992, the SAAB 2000 was a stretched version of the SAAB 340. With an extension of 23ft 11in (7.28m), it could now seat 50 passengers. Power was from two 4125shp Allison AE2100A turboprops. Pictured in June 1998 at Tampere-Pirkkala Airport, Finland, is SAAB 2000 SE-LSE c/n 2000-046 in the colours of Scandinavian Commuter, Swedlink. They were, at first, a division of Scandinavian Airlines and later absorbed into the main company. This aircraft was sold on and was in store in Alaska in 2018.

The Dornier 228 had a very distinctive wing shape. It was a commuter airliner that first flew in March 1981 and could seat 19 passengers. Power came from a pair of Garrett TPE331-5 turboprops with an output of 776shp. Pictured against the blue sky at Athens International Airport, in June 1993, is Dornier Do.228-201 SX-BHE c/n 8050 of Olympic Aviation. The aircraft was sold on and now operates in Kenya.

Pictured in November 1992 at Kavac, Venezuela, is Dornier Do.228-212 YV-534C c/n 8184 of Caracas-based carrier, Aereotuy. It was on a charter to bring tourists to see Angel Falls, the world's tallest waterfall. Aereotuy were later rebranded LTA (Línea Turistica Aereotuy); they ceased operations in June 2018, with plans to restart at a later date. This aircraft is still with them but in storage.

Dornier flew the follow-up to the 228 in December 1991. This new model was called the Dornier 328. It was a new turboprop powered by a pair of Pratt & Whitney PW119B engines and held seating for 31 passengers. Pictured in September 1997 at Mariscal Sucre International Airport, Ecuador, is Dornier Do.328-120 HC-BXO c/n 3076 of Club VIP (Vuelos Internos Privados). They had started as a charter company flying for members only. In 2012, they merged with Aerogal. This aircraft was withdrawn from use and broken up in Opa Locka, Florida, in 2007.

In 1943, Vultee Aircraft merged with Consolidated Aircraft to form Consolidated Vultee; in 1947, this was shortened to Convair. With World War Two over, the company wanted to build a new non-military airliner. In 1946, the company flew the Convair 110, but this aircraft was considered too small. The Convair 240 (with two engines and a configuration for up to 40 passengers) followed shortly after. It was piston powered with a pair of Pratt & Whitney R-2800 radials with an output of 2400hp each. Seen in November 1992 on the ramp at Luis Muñoz Marín International Airport, San Juan, is Convair 240 N355T c/n 281 of Dodita Air Cargo. They had started in 1990 and closed down operations in 2006. This aircraft was written off in May 1997 in Luquillo, Puerto Rico. The engines failed and the aircraft landed on a beach, stopping in five feet of water.

The manufacturer stretched the Convair 240 by 4ft 6in (1.37m) and it became the Convair 340. Pictured in November 1992 at La Paz International Airport, Bolivia, is Convair 340 CP-2026 c/n 249 of CAT (Cargo Aero Transportada). In this picture, the aircraft is undergoing maintenance and one of its engines has been removed. The company was one of the meat haulers from the lowland farms to the city of La Paz, which sat 12,000ft (3657m) above sea level. This aircraft is still listed as currently in service in Bolivia.

Pictured in November 1992 on the ramp at Jorge Wilstermann Airport, Cochabamba, is Convair 340 CP-2236 c/n 215 of locally based LAC (Líneas Aéreas Canedo), who operated spotless aircraft and still do. This aircraft was sold to Rovos Air, a South African luxury travel company. It was then sold to a Dutch company who planned to fly this aircraft back to Europe and place it in a museum. However, in July 2018, whilst on a test flight from Wonderboom, South Africa, it had an engine fire and crashed into a built-up area with fatal results.

In comparison to the Convair 340, the Convair 440 had a lengthened radar nose and longer engine nacelles. It could also seat up to 52 passengers. Pictured in June 1990 on the ramp at Willow Run Airport, Detroit, is Convair 440 N323CF c/n 323 of locally based Trans Continental Airlines. They were an all-cargo carrier who ceased operations in 1999, but reformed in Naples, Florida, as Express.net Airlines. This aircraft was sold on to a company in Florida and withdrawn in 2006.

Pictured in November 1992 on the ramp at Santo Domingo, Dominican Republic, is Convair 440 HI-594CT c/n 118 of locally based TRADO (Trans Dominican Airways). While this carrier flew a mix of passengers and cargo, this aircraft was configured for 44 people. They suspended operations in 1997 and this aircraft was stored and broken up in 2003.

The Convair 340 and 440 airframes were able to be updated with the replacement of the piston engines with 3750shp Allison 501 turboprops. This work was done by Pac Aero and the first conversion took place in 1960; the converted aircraft were known as Convair 580. Pictured in October 1998 at Avra Valley Airport, Arizona, is Convair 580 N73301 c/n 80 of Tucson-based Sierra Pacific Airlines. They started operations in 1976 and today fly Boeing 737s. This aircraft was sold on to Conair Aviation of Abbotsford, Canada, who converted it to an air tanker for fighting forest fires. It was damaged beyond repair in Manning, Alberta, in May 2016; following a landing accident and runway excursion, the fuselage broke into two sections.

While some Convair models, such as the 340 and 440, received an updated Allison turboprop engine, other models were re-engined with Rolls-Royce Darts. This latter version was named the 640. Pictured in June 1990 at Willow Run Airport, Detroit, is Convair 640 N7529U c/n 58 of Zantop International Airlines. This aircraft was broken up and the registration cancelled in 2002.

One could call the Curtiss C-46 Commando the 'tramp steamer of the skies' or liken this propliner to a workhorse. It was the same layout as the Dakota but was much larger. Piston-powered, it had a pair of 2,000hp Pratt & Whitney R-2800 air-cooled radials. By the 1990s, these aircraft were only to be found in South America, Northern Canada and Alaska. Pictured in June 1990 at Oxford House, Manitoba, is Curtiss C-46 Commando C-GTXW c/n 30386 operated by Winnipeg-based Northland Air Manitoba. This airline flew both freight and passenger services and, on the day of photographing, this C-46 was delivering assorted goods to First Nation settlements. The company suspended operations in 1997. This aircraft was sold on and was written off in September 2015 in Déline, North West Territory, after an engine fire and a belly landing.

By the 1990s, two countries in South America, Bolivia and Colombia, accounted for all the C-46 activity in that continent. Seen in September 1997 at La Vanguardia Airport, Villavicencio, is Curtiss C-46A Commando HK-851 c/n 383 of locally based Coral (Coronado Aerolineas). They ceased operations in 2000 and this aircraft was sold on. In 2000, a short distance from Villavicencio, this aircraft crashed. Following a fire after take-off, the overloaded aircraft impacted with the ground resulting in ten fatalities. The aircraft was, at the time of crashing, owned by an individual not an airline.

Pictured with the engines running on the ramp at La Paz International Airport, Bolivia, in November 1992, is Curtiss C-46A Commando CP-746 c/n 26417 of Universal Transportes Aéreos. They were one of the companies who flew freshly killed meat from the outer-lying farms into the city. The company was renamed SAO (Servicios Aéreos del Oriente). This aircraft was written off when serving with SAO, in July 1999, following a landing accident at an unknown location in Bolivia.

Seen in November 1992 with its large freight door open, at the company base of Jorge Wilstermann International Airport, Cochabamba, Bolivia, is Curtiss C-46F Commando CP-1616 c/n 22501. It is dressed in the livery of North East Bolivian Airways. They were a general cargo company who operated with just two aircraft. They ceased operations in 2006. This aircraft was engineless and parked out in long grass in Trinidad, Bolivia, in 2013.

All of the big three Douglas Aircraft Company four-engine piston powered transports – the DC-4, DC-6 and DC-7 – could be found in service during the 1990s, albeit in very reduced numbers. The Douglas DC-4 was powered by Pratt & Whitney R-2000 Twin Wasp air-cooled radial piston engines. The bulk of the production centred around the Douglas C-54 Skymaster, which were first manufactured during World War Two for military purposes and with a large cargo door; these were the ones most likely to be found still in service. Pictured at Borinquen, Puerto Rico, in November 1992, is Douglas C-54 N4989K c/n 27319 of Pontiac, Michigan-based carrier, Contract Air Cargo. It shows how smart some of these old aircraft can be. The company is now part of the IFL Group; this aircraft was sold to a company in South Africa and, by 2017, was derelict at Rand Airport, Johannesburg.

Seen on the ramp at the company base of Toronto Pearson International Airport, in June 1990, is Douglas C-54 C-GQIB c/n 27370 of Millardair. The company took its name from the founder, Carl Millard, and was a general cargo operator. In 1990, this carrier closed down operations. This aircraft was sold to the Berlin Airlift Historic Foundation who took it to air shows around the United States. Sadly, it was damaged beyond economic repair in Walterboro, South Carolina, in April 2020, during a tornado. A replacement has been found to carry on the foundation's work.

The Douglas DC-6 was the next of the four-engine Douglas Aircraft Company aircraft; it first flew in June 1946 and was powered by 2100hp Pratt & Whitney R-2800 Double Wasp radials. It was built for both civil and military operators. Seen in November 1992 on the ramp at La Paz International Airport, Bolivia, is Douglas DC-6A CP-1282 c/n 45530 of La Transportes Aéreas la Cumbre, a local meat hauler. The meat flights would see the aircraft take off from the city of La Paz and fly to lowland farms. While the aircraft was approaching, cattle would be brought in at the farm and slaughtered; the freshly killed carcasses would be loaded on to the aircraft and it would fly back to La Paz. Upon arrival, open trucks would take the meat to local markets. It is worth noting that the word refrigeration has not been used. As can be seen in this picture, corporate image was not top priority for these carriers. The company closed down operations in 1995; the aircraft was withdrawn and has been in store at La Paz since then.

With a fleet of just one aircraft, CAN (Companie Aérea Nacional) were a La Paz-based meat hauler. Pictured on their ramp at base, in November 1992, is Douglas DC-6 CP-1654 c/n 43035. In this picture, the large freight door is open and they are cleaning out the aircraft after collecting freshly killed cattle to bring to the city. A stream of water, blood and offal can be seen pouring onto the ground. This always proved a treat to local dogs, which would rush to lick it up. This aircraft crashed in March 1993 in Santa Rosa, Bolivia, when the number two engine caught fire on take-off. The pilot aborted the run but it overran the runway and was destroyed. Since the company only had one aircraft, they were forced to cease operations.

The United Kingdom was lucky enough to have an operator that flew the classic Douglas Aircraft propliner. Pictured at its base at Coventry Airport, in April 1991, is Douglas DC-6A G-APSA c/n 45497 of Air Atlantique. They flew general cargo as required around Europe. This aircraft was repainted in vintage British Eagle International Airline colours for work in films and in air shows. During 2021, it is due to go to MOD St Athan to be part of the display at South Wales Aviation Museum.

Seen in June 1990 on the ramp at Willow Run Airport, Detroit, is Douglas DC-6A N615SE c/n 43296 in the smart livery of Trans Continental Airlines. The bulk of the cargo operations for this airline were associated with the large motor industry in the area. This aircraft was broken up for spare parts in Fairbanks, Alaska, following its sale in 1998.

The last of the three Douglas Aircraft Company four-engine propliners was the largest; the DC-7 first flew in May 1953 and was powered by Wright R-3350 3250hp turbo-compound radial engines. Pictured at Las Américas International Airport in Santo Domingo, Dominican Republic, in November 1992, is Douglas DC-7C HR-ALY c/n 45230 owned by Aero Servicios. This smartly painted aircraft was written off at Miami International Airport, in March 1994, when a fuel tank exploded during maintenance. It was broken up in February the following year.

In the early 1990s, Santo Domingo, Dominican Republic, was a hot bed of classic piston operators. Douglas DC-7CF HI-599CT c/n 45208 of Aerochago is seen at Las Américas International Airport in November 1992. Sadly, in February of the following year the aircraft was written off here when an engine failed on take-off; it ran off the runway and the damage was deemed beyond economic repair. The company ceased operations in 2004.

As well as the DC-7, Aerochago also operated a most elegant aircraft, the Lockheed Constellation. The Santo Domingo base was the last place to see the type in working mode as a cargo aircraft. On the ramp, in November 1992, is Lockheed L-1049F Super Constellation HI-548 c/n 4202. Sadly, it was broken up here in 1999.

It is unlikely that, for the foreseeable future, there will be a decade of aviation history that fails to feature a Douglas DC-3. Many aircraft have been designed and built to replace them, but history has shown that the only DC-3 replacement is, in fact, another DC-3. Pictured with its Pratt & Whitney R-1830 radial pistons running at Olaya Herrera Airport in Medellin, Colombia, in November 1992, is Douglas DC-3 Dakota HK-1212 c/n 4987 of Sadelca (Sociedad Aérea de Caquetá), an all-freight company then based at Neiva. They have moved now to La Vanguardia Airport, Villavicencio. This aircraft was sold on and written off in June 2004 at Las Gaviotas Airport, Colombia. During a take-off run, the right-hand engine failed and it crashed into trees and caught fire. Luckily, there was no loss of life amongst the 20 people on board.

Based in Winnipeg, Manitoba, Northland Air Manitoba flew both passenger and cargo models of the DC-3s. On the ramp at base, in June 1990, is Douglas DC-3 Dakota C-FIKD c/n 33569. This was one of six DC-3s operated by the airline at that time; this one is equipped with 27 seats for passengers. This aircraft was sold on and is currently in California with private owners who fly it with Classic Airways markings. The company dropped the Northland name to become Air Manitoba the following year and ceased their own operations in 1997. They then operated as a leasing company.

The Virgin Group of companies have had few business failures. However, one notable exception was the Virgin Group subsidiary of Vintage Airways. The idea was to fly from its Kissimmee Gateway Airport base to Key West International Airport in a period aircraft. Its passengers were to be told it was 1945 and various props of magazines and crew outfits were designed to highlight this. Sadly, not enough interest was shown and operations were suspended in October 1994. Pictured at its base, in April 1994, is Douglas DC-3 Dakota N22RB c/n 4926. This aircraft was damaged beyond repair at Orlando Executive Airfield at Herndon when, in August 2004, Hurricane Charley blew the aircraft onto its back.

Pictured against the wonderful backdrop of Kavac, central Venezuela, in November 1992, is Douglas DC-3 Dakota YV-218C c/n 43079 of Rutaca (Rutas Aéreas Compania Anonima). It had brought tourists to see the world's tallest waterfall, Angel Falls. This aircraft had been put into store at the company base at Tomás de Heres Airport, Ciudad Bolivar, by 2001.

Pictured is a typical South American scene in which passengers exit a Douglas DC-3 with just a small ladder. It will have carried both cargo and passengers at the same time. The location is La Vanguardia Airport, Villavicencio, in November 1992 and the aircraft is Douglas DC-3 Dakota HK-2213 c/n 11752 operated by Transoriente. They later replaced the DC-3 with Dornier Skyservants. This aircraft was damaged beyond repair following a double engine failure and a forced landing.

Pictured in September 1997 at La Vanguardia Airport, Villavicencio, is Douglas DC-3 Dakota HK-122 c/n 4414 of Lineas Aéreas El Dorado. Locally based, this airliner closed two years later. Sold on, this aircraft had an unhappy ending in July 2011 in La Mosquita, Honduras. It was set ablaze by drug dealers following a structural failure from its overweight cargo of three tons of cocaine.

Shot from the control tower of La Vanguardia Airport, Villavicencio, in September 1997, is a plan view of Douglas DC-3 Dakota HK-3293 c/n 9186 of Air Colombia. In July 2018, this aircraft was badly damaged in San Felipe, Colombia, in a runway excursion and ended up in a ditch that caused a fire in the left engine. It was undergoing a rebuild in Villavicencio when the company closed down in September 2019.

Douglas produced their own Dakota replacement and, initially, sold just three to the airlines. It was saved by an order for 100 from the United States Navy, which gave it the designation R4D-8 (later C-117). There was, of course, nothing wrong with the aircraft itself but, at the end of World War Two, there were too many surplus C-47/DC-3 Dakotas far cheaper than a new type. The Super Dakota, as it was called, could be recognised by the tall tail. Seen at its Toronto base, in June 1990, is Douglas C-117D Super Dakota C-FALL c/n 43385 of Air 500. The company closed in 2004 and this aircraft went south to Florida in 1998. It was in a poor state at Fort Lauderdale when it was broken up, with the nose section being preserved at the Wings over Miami Military and Classic Aircraft Museum. The registration was cancelled by the Federal Aviation Administration (FAA) in September 2013.

Not all passenger flights take place at large airports with giant jetliners. A smaller, yet equally important, strand of aviation takes place in remote areas of the world with small aircraft. The ultimate 'bush' aircraft has to be the de Havilland Canada DHC-2 Beaver. During the design process, de Havilland reached out to their potential customers to ask what they needed. One simple requirement was a door wide enough to take a fuel drum. The completed aircraft first flew in August 1947 and can operate on wheels, skis or floats. Power is from a single 450hp Pratt & Whitney Wasp Junior radial piston engine. Pictured in June 1990 at Sioux Lookout Sea Plane Base, Ontario, is de Havilland DHC-2 Beaver C-FHEP c/n 69 of Sioux Air. This aircraft is now in store at Sioux Lookout Airport, on wheels and without an engine. Its registration was cancelled in 2005, however, if it is needed, it could always be put back into service.

Following the Beaver came the DHC-3 Otter; it first flew in December 1951 and had a 600hp Pratt & Whitney Wasp R-1340 radial piston engine. Pictured on Rainy Lake, Ontario, in June 1990, is de Havilland Canada DHC-3 Otter C-GUTL c/n 365 of Northern Wilderness Outfitters. A large tourist industry in Ontario is to take fishermen to remote lake-side lodges for a week of secluded fishing. The only access to such places is by float plane. The carrier still operates from their base at Rainy Lake SPB; this aircraft has been re-engined with a P&W PT-6A to make it a Turbo Otter. It currently serves with a company operating in Fort Francis, Ontario.

Predating the DHC-2 Beaver by a decade was the Noorduyn Norseman. Bob Noorduyn started the design work in 1934, and it first flew, in November 1935, from the St Lawrence River as a float plane. It took a few engine fits before they settled with the 550hp Pratt & Whitney Wasp R-1340. Production ran until 1959 and, by that time, over 900 aircraft had been built. Pictured, in June 1990, is Noorduyn Norseman VI C-FJEC c/n 469 of Sabourin Lake Airways on its take off run from Sabourin Lake, Ontario. The company operated a mixed fleet from their base at Red Lake Airport, Cochenour, before suspending operations in 1996. This classic aircraft is now with a private owner in Quebec.

With a production run from 1937 to 1969, the Beechcraft Model 18 can today still be found in various operations. Pictured over the Fort Francis area of Ontario, in June 1990, is Beech 18 C-FERM c/n CA-62 of Rusty Myers Flying Services, based at Fort Frances Sea Plane Base. Note the large ventral fin; this is to offset the extra side area of the EDO floats. This aircraft is still in service with the company. The camera ship was another of the company's Beech 18s.

As in the Western world, during the late 1950s, designers in the USSR were working on twin-turboprops to replace their old piston-powered aircraft. These were the Ilyushin IL-14 and the Lisunov Li-2. This latter aircraft was a licence-built version of the DC-3. The Kiev-based Antonov OKB (Design Bureau) came up with the Antonov An-24. First flown in December 1962, it was powered by a pair of 2,550shp Ivchenko IA-24V turboprops and could seat up to 50 passengers. Pictured in March 1997 at Sharjah International Airport, UAE, is Antonov An-24RV EL-AKO c/n 57310206 of local carrier, Air Cess. The An-24RV variant of the An-24 had been designed for hot and high operations; in the rear of the right hand engine nacelle a 1,980lb st Tumanskii RV-19-300 jet engine had been fitted. Air Cess was rebranded as Air Bas in 2001 and this aircraft is in store in Brazzaville, Republic of Congo.

To make a full cargo version of the An-24, the manufacturer produced the An-26. This aircraft had a rear loading ramp with drive-in capability. Pictured at Liverpool Airport, in June 1993, is Antonov An-26 YL-RAC c/n 9903 of Riga, Latvia-based RAF Avia. They still operate and own this aircraft, however, it has since been leased to another freight operator.

The ultimate variant of the An-24 was the Antonov An-32. The size of the new engines and the required propellers meant that the new power plants had to be mounted on top of the wing. The new units were 5,180shp Ivchenko AI-20M turboprops, which had nearly twice the power of the original An-24. Seen in September 1997 at La Vanguardia Airport, Villavicencio, is Antonov An-32 HK-4117X c/n 2909 of Sadelca. This aircraft was written off in August 2007 in Mitú, Colombia; the aircraft had been delivering a cargo of fuel and suffered a spillage. When the auxiliary power unit and the number two engine were started there was an explosion and the airframe was consumed by fire.

The Xian Y-7 is an Antonov An-24 built, under licence, by Chinese manufacturer Xi'an Aircraft Industrial Corporation. Seen in October 1999 at Xi'an Xianyang International Airport, China, is Xian Y-7-200A B-3720 c/n 0001 of local carrier, Changan Air. The -200 version of the Xian Y-7 has Pratt & Whitney Canada PW-150A turboprops fitted for better performance and fuel economy. The carrier now operates as Chang'An Airlines and this aircraft has been withdrawn from service.

Designed as a military freighter, the Antonov An-8, first flew in 1955. The aircraft was one of the first to have a ventral rear loading ramp that allowed vehicles to drive in. Power was from a pair of Ivchenko AI-20 turboprops. It was first believed that all of this type had been withdrawn by the start of the 1990s, but they started to appear out of the USSR as the state dissolved. Seen in March 1997 at Sharjah International Airport, UAE, is Antonov An-8 EL-AKZ c/n OD.3450 of Santa Cruz Imperial Airlines. They suspended operation in 2008 and this aircraft had been broken up here in 2004.

First flown in October 1966, the Yakovlev Yak-40 was a regional airliner that could seat up to 32 passengers. Power was from a trio of 3,300lb st Ivchenko AI-25 turbofans. Pictured in August 1991 at Kiev-Zhulyany, is Yakovlev Yak-40 CCCP-87841 c/n 9330930 of the USSR's state carrier Aeroflot. In fact, all civil aircraft at that time in the country came under the umbrella Aeroflot. Following the demise of the USSR, this aircraft stayed in the Ukraine and had the Soviet Union registration replaced by the new 'UR' of the now independent nation. It operated with the airline Dniproavia, was withdrawn at Dnepropetrovsk International Airport in 1999, and was last noted in 2013 in poor condition with faded colours.

The Yak-40s, and the airlines that operated them, are a very good example of how much could change in a few short years and how new non-Aeroflot airlines could develop. Pictured in August 1995 at Bykovo Airport, Moscow, is Yakovlev Yak-40 RA-21505 c/n 9830159 of Nadym Airlines. They were formed in the town of Nadym in the Tyumen Oblast region of Russia. Nadym Airlines were taken over by Gazpromavia Airlines; this aircraft was sold on and is still currently in use.

The Yakovlev Yak-42 was a medium-range airliner first flown in March 1975. It was powered by three mounted 14,325lb st Ivchenko D-36 turbofans – two on the rear fuselage and one at the base of the fin. Pictured at Düsseldorf International Airport, in September 1998, is Yakovlev Yak-42 T9-ABC c/n 11151004 of Air Bosna from Sarajevo, Bosnia-Herzegovina, one of the new nations that emerged from the civil war and breakup of Yugoslavia. The airline closed operations in June 2005 and this aircraft had been returned to the leasing company during 1999. It was later withdrawn from use in Lvov, Ukraine, in 2007.

One of the effects of the breakup of the USSR and Aeroflot as a monopoly was the vast number of airlines that were formed all over the huge landmass that once made up the USSR. Pictured at Frankfurt Airport, in June 1999, is Yakovlev Yak-42D RA-42367 c/n 4520421914133 of Kuban Airlines, travelling from their base at Krasnodar International Airport. The carrier closed down in December 2012 and this aircraft was put into store at their base.

Seen in August 1995 at Bykovo Airport, Moscow, is Yakovlev Yak-42 RA-42324 c/n 4520421402125 of Bykovo Avia. Three of the four Moscow airports operating in this decade held airlines that used the airport name as their operating name. They had once been the Aeroflot Bykovo Division, however, in 1999, they were merged into Centre-Avia Airlines. This aircraft was broken up in 2008 and the airline ceased operations in 2010.

Pictured on the ramp following a scheduled passenger service to Santo Domingo, Dominican Republic, in November 1992, is Yakovlev Yak-42D CU-T1277 c/n 4520423016238 of Havana-based, flag carrying airline, Cubana. It was configured to hold 120 passengers in an all-economy class and has since been put into store.

On the move at Frankfurt Airport, in June 1999, is Yakovlev Yak-42D UR-42426 c/n 4520423304016 of Dnepropetrovsk-based airline, Dniproavia (a subsidiary of Air Ukraine). Their fleet, at that time, was made up of Yak-40s and 42s. This aircraft had a two-class seating configuration of 12 business and 84 economy. The company ceased operations in 2013; this aircraft was sold on and, in 2018, was broken up in Khartoum, Sudan.

In the Western world, the standard military transporter was the Lockheed C-130 Hercules. Alternatively, in the communist and non-aligned nations, the Antonov An-12 was the preferred option. It first flew in December 1957 and was powered by four 4000shp Kuznetsov NK-4 turboprops, with later versions having Ivchenko AI-20A engines. Pictured in March 1997 at Sharjah International Airport, UAE, is Antonov An-12 RA-11325 c/n 5342801 of Polet Airlines – Rossijskaya Aviakompania, who were based in Voronezh, Central Russia. They suspended operations in November 2014. This aircraft was sold to an operator in Afghanistan in February 1998 and, in October 2001, was destroyed by the US bombing of Kabul, following the 9/11 attacks on the United States.

Photographed in March 1997 at Sharjah International Airport, UAE, is Antonov An-12 EL-RDL c/n 2340809 of locally based Air Cess. They had a name change to Air Bas in 2001. This aircraft was sold to a company in Africa and later put in store in Ras Al Khaimah, UAE.

China has often licence built aircraft designed in the USSR. Their version of the An-12 was the Y-8. The development of this aircraft in China was very slow as the effects of the Cultural Revolution had slowed work, and the production location was changed from Xian to the Shaanxi Transport Aircraft Factory at Hanchung. The first Y-8 flew in December 1974 and was powered by four Zhuzhou Engine Factory WJ-6 turboprops. This engine was the result of reverse engineering a Russian-built AI-20K power plant. The main visual difference between the Russian and Chinese machines was that the Chinese ones had a longer nose. This was the same one fitted to the Xian H-6 bomber, which was itself a copy of the Soviet-era Tupolev Tu-16. Pictured in October 1999 at Guangzhou Airport, is Yunshuji Y-8F-100 B-3102 c/n 50805 of China Postal Airlines. Based in Tianjin, they fly for the government's Ministry of Posts. This aircraft is still currently with them.

First flown in December 1982, the Antonov An-124 Ruslan is a very large civil and military freighter powered by four Lotarev D-18T turbofans with an output of 51,590lb st. It captured the civil market through its ability to move outsized or heavy loads. It is the only aircraft that can be hired for these jobs other than the solitary six-engine Antonov An-225 produced. Pictured in March 1997 at Sharjah International Airport, UAE, is Antonov An-124-100 Ruslan RA-82078 c/n 9773054559153 of Ulyanovsk-based Volga-Dnepr Airlines, an all-freight carrier. This aircraft still serves with the company.

While the Western world had the Lockheed Electra and the Bristol Britannia, the USSR had the Ilyushin IL-18. It first flew in July 1957 and was powered by four turboprops. It had a longer front-line service than the two aforementioned Western aircrafts, as their operators bowed to customer demands for pure jets instead of turboprops. However, in the USSR, 'customer choice' was not of the greatest concern to Aeroflot. Pictured on the ramp, in August 1995, at its base is Ilyushin IL-18D RA-74268 c/n 18811201 of Domodedovo Airlines. It was one of three airlines named after the Moscow-based airport from which they flew from. The company closed down in November 2008 and this aircraft moved to a carrier in Kyrgyzstan.

Interflug was the airline of the old East German state. When the Berlin Wall came down in November 1989, this airline could no longer compete with the well-established airlines of Europe and so ceased operations in October 1990. Pictured in July 1991 at RAF Fairford, Gloucestershire, is Ilyushin IL-18D D-AOAU c/n 188010904. It is still in Interflug livery but is being operated by Berline, which was offering cash-in-hand pleasure flights. This aircraft was sold to a carrier in Cuba and later broken up.

The Ilyushin IL-86 was the first Soviet wide-bodied aircraft. It first took to the air in December 1976 and was powered by four Samara NK-86 turbofans with an output of 29,320lb st. Unfortunately, these engines left it underpowered. Pictured on arrival at Frankfurt Airport, in June 1999, is Ilyushin IL-86 RA-86106 c/n 51483208074 of Pulkovo Airlines. This carrier is named after its base at Pulkovo Airport, St Petersburg. The company merged with Rossiya Airlines in October 2006 and this aircraft was sold that year. It was stored at Pulkovo in 2008, with the engines removed, with the intention of using it as a cabin trainer.

Pictured in September 1995 on the runway at Sheremetyevo International Airport, Moscow, is Ilyushin IL-86 RA-86145 c/n 51483211101 of AJT Air International (Asian Joint Transport). Their fleet of Ilyushin-built IL-86s were all configured to have an all-economy, 350 seat layout. The company closed down in 2003 and this aircraft was sold on and later broken up.

Taking off from its base at Ürümqi Diwopu International Airport base in the far west of China, in October 1999, is Ilyushin IL-86 B-2018 c/n 51483210099 of China Xinjiang Airlines. They were taken over by China Southern Airlines in 2004. This aircraft went to a Russian company and was later stored in Domodedovo, Moscow. It was broken up at the end of 2010.

To solve some of the lack of power in the IL-86, the manufacturer produced the IL-96. It had more powerful Aviadvigatel PS-90A turbofans with an output of 35,275lb st. Additionally a new wing was fitted that included winglets and the fuselage was reduced by 29ft 3in (8.91m). Seen in September 1995 at Sheremetyevo International Airport, Moscow, is Ilyushin IL-96-300 RA-96008 c/n 74393201005 of Russia's state airline Aeroflot. It was sold to Cuba in September 2014, withdrawn four years later and stored at Havana.

First flown in January 1961, the Ilyushin IL-62 was a long-range airliner with four rear mounted engines. The IL-62M had extra fuel tanks in the fin and Soloviev D-30KU turbofans. Pictured at its home base of Domodedovo Moscow Airport, in August 1995, is Ilyushin IL-62M RA-86501 c/n 3933121 of Domodedovo Airlines. This aircraft was broken up here in October 1999.

Pictured in September 1995 at Sheremetyevo International Airport, Moscow, is Ilyushin IL-62M RA-86567 c/n 4256314 of locally based carrier, Orient Avia. They started operations in 1994, with services to the far eastern areas of Russia and went bankrupt in July 1997. This aircraft was sold on, stored at Magadan in 2008 and broken up in March 2015.

Pictured in November 1999 at Bangkok, Thailand, is Ilyushin IL-62M P-881 c/n 3647853 of Air Koryo. They are the sole airline in the Democratic People's Republic of Korea (DPRK), more commonly known as North Korea. They operate from the capital Pyongyang and run a very irregular service schedule. This aircraft was withdrawn and stored at their base in September 2015.

Seen in August 1995 at Zhukovsky airfield, Moscow, is Ilyushin IL-62M UN-86130 c/n 3255333 of Aral Air from Kazakhstan. The company ceased operations and this USSR-built aircraft was sold on. By 2009, this aircraft was in store at Tehran. The 'UN' country registration prefix has since been changed to 'UP' as the original was sometimes confused with United Nations operations.

One of the most widely used and versatile cargo aircraft is the Ilyushin IL-76. It first flew in March 1971 and is powered by four Soloviev D-30KP turbofans with an output of 26,455lb st. Pictured in August 1991 at Pulkovo Airport, Leningrad, is Ilyushin IL-76 CCCP-78805 c/n 0093492783. As all USSR-based civil aircraft were at that time, it is operated by, and in the colours of, Aeroflot. This aircraft is now in service with the Russian Air Force.

Uzbekistan was one of the new countries to emerge from the breakup of the USSR in 1991. Seen in March 1997 at Sharjah International Airport, UAE, is Ilyushin IL-76TD UK-76793 c/n 0093498951 of Uzbekistan Airways. Based in Tashkent, they currently have a mixed fleet of Western and Soviet built equipment. This aircraft was put in store, at base, in 2006.

One of the many new carriers created in Russia – with a notably excellent colour scheme – was Avia Energo, which was based at Sheremetyevo International Airport, Moscow. They were a subsidiary of the United Energy System of Russia and their role was to handle the logistic needs of the company. They acted as a general charter company and operated several types of aircraft configured for both passenger and cargo. Pictured in March 1997 at Sharjah International Airport, UAE, is Ilyushin IL-76 RA-76366 c/n 1043418628. Services were suspended in June 2011 because of a poor financial performance. This aircraft now operates with another Russian carrier.

The Ilyushin IL-78 was an adaptation of the Ilyushin IL-76 and was manufactured as a military in-flight refuelling tanker. Seen in March 1997 at Sharjah International Airport, UAE, is Ilyushin IL-78 UR-76689 c/n 0063469066 of Kiev-based BSL Airlines. They ceased operations the following year. This aircraft had quite a mixed history; it was built as a tanker, however, in 1995, the tanking equipment was removed and it operated as a normal freighter. From there, it was later put in store until 2013. Three years later, it was reconverted back into a tanker and sold to China to join the People's Liberation Army Air Force.

The Tupolev Tu-134 was first flown in July 1963. Its role was as a short-haul airliner. Power came from a pair of rear-mounted Soloviev D-30 turbofans with an output of 14,990lb st. Pictured in August 1991 from the control tower at Leningrad-Pulkovo Airport, is Tupolev Tu-134A-3 CCCP-65837 c/n 17114 of Aeroflot. The -134A had a 6ft 11in (2.1m) fuselage stretch and seating for 76 passengers in one class. This aircraft stayed in the area and joined Pulkovo Avia; it was withdrawn from use in 1997 and then broken up.

Another of the new airlines of Russia is seen in March 1997 at Sharjah International Airport, UAE. It is Tupolev Tu-134A-3 RA-65983 c/n 63350 of Permtransavia. Based in the city of Perm, they were the flying division of the Perm Motors Corporation. They flew both corporate and charter services and were later rebranded as Permskie Motory Avia Kompania and suspended operations in 2002. This was the only one to wear the airline's full colours. It was sold on in 1998 and used by two carriers in Russia before being stored.

Climbing out of Sharjah International Airport, UAE, in March 1997 is Tupolev Tu-134B-3 YL-LBE c/n 63285 of Riga, Latvia-based LAT Charter. The carrier's home nation of Latvia is one of three Baltic Republics who once again became independent following the demise of the USSR. The carrier was renamed Smart Lynx in September 2008. This aircraft was sold to a leasing company in 2003 and registered in Kazakhstan.

The country of Georgia was one of the former USSR states that became independent; with this independence came the new aircraft registration of '4L'. Seen on arrival in August 1995 at Vnukovo International Airport, Moscow, is Tupolev Tu-134A-3 4L-65061 c/n 49874 of Adjal Avia (Adjarian Airlines). Based in Batumi, Georgia, some of the carrier's fleet of Tu-134s operated under the marketing name of the brand, Taifun. The carrier was later renamed Batumi Adjarian Airlines. This aircraft was sold on, put into store and later broken up.

First flown in October 1968, the Tupolev Tu-154 was a medium-range airliner. It was powered by three Kuznetsov NK-8 turbofans, with two mounted on the rear fuselage and one at the base of the fin. The Tupolev Design Bureau reported that, in the early part of the 1990s, half of all passenger travel in the USSR was on the Tu-154. Following the demise of the USSR and the end of the Aeroflot monopoly, most of the new airlines and countries kept this type of aircraft in service. Seen on the ramp at Moscow Domodedovo Airport, in August 1995, is Tupolev Tu-154B RA-85112 c/n 112 of Bashkirian Airlines. They were based in the city of Ufa, which was in the autonomous Republic of Bashkortostan. They suspended operations in 2007 and this aircraft was withdrawn from service in September 1997 in Ufa and broken up.

With the liberation and establishment of a new country came new aircraft registration letters. Seen in March 1997 at Sharjah International Airport, UAE, is Tupolev Tu-154B-2 EY-85475 c/n 475 of Tajik Air. Based in Dushanbe, Tajikistan, the carrier, who is still operates, withdrew this aircraft in 2007 and it was later broken up.

Most of the new states from the old USSR painted their fleets in smart colour schemes. Pictured in March 1997 at Sharjah International Airport, UAE, is Tupolev Tu-154B-2 UN-85396 c/n 396 of Kazakhstan Airlines. They suspended operations for a time and later returned as Air Kazakhstan. This aircraft was withdrawn by 2002 at Almaty.

Pictured upon arrival at Frankfurt Airport, in June 1997, is Tupolev Tu-154B-2 4L-85547 c/n 547 of Air Georgia. In November 1999, the carrier merged with Airzena to form Airzena Georgian Airways. This aircraft was configured in a three-class layout with 12 first, 18 business and 104 economy seats. It later received the new registration of 4L-AAG. It was stored and then broken up at the company base of Tbilisi.

Looking smarter in this photograph than it ever did in an Aeroflot livery is Tupolev Tu-154B-2 RA-85508 c/n 508 of Ural Airlines. It was pictured at Sharjah International Airport, UAE, in March 1997. Once the Sverdlovsk division of Aeroflot, Ural Airlines were based in Ekaterinburg, from where they continue to operate. This aircraft held a one-class configuration with seating for 164 all-economy passengers. The aircraft was withdrawn from service and broken up; the company now has an all-Airbus fleet.

Pictured on its landing approach to Frankfurt Airport, in June 1997, is Tupolev Tu-154M EX-85762 c/n 945 of Kyrghyzstan Airlines. As can be seen, this aircraft is still in a basic Aeroflot colour scheme with just the titles and registration changed. The company was based in Bishkek in the new country of the Kyrgyz Republic and was declared bankrupt in 2005. This aircraft joined the nation's government, got a new VIP livery and interior and is still in operation.

Yet another attractive smart colour scheme is on view at Frankfurt Airport, in June 1999. It is Tupolev Tu-154M UN-85782 c/n 966 of Vipair, based in Astana International Airport, Kazakhstan. They suspended operations later that year; there was an intention to restart and their fleet of two Tu-154s were put in store at base. This aircraft was sold to a Russian carrier in 2005.

Of all of the new nations that grew from the dissolution of the USSR, the most advanced was the Ukraine. Pictured at Beijing, in October 1999, is Tupolev Tu-154M UR-85707 c/n 882 of Air Ukraine. Based in Kiev, Air Ukraine were the former Aeroflot Kiev Directorate. Operations were suspended in 2003 and this aircraft was sold to a Russian carrier in 2009. It is now in store.

One of the most attractive colours schemes to grace a Tu-154 has to be the one pictured in August 1995 at Vnukovo International Airport, Moscow. It is Tupolev Tu-154 RA-85619 c/n 738 in the livery of Meta Aviotransport Macedonia. The Skopje-based company had leased it from Vnukovo Airways, but they had suspended operation in January of the previous year. This aircraft went back to work with Vnukovo Airways, who were taken over by Sibir Airlines in 2001, and this aircraft joined their fleet. The Siberian carrier was based in Novosibirsk, southern Russia, and, following rebranding, now operates today as S7 Airlines. It was withdrawn from use in 2008 and broken up four years later. In an interesting footnote to this aircraft's history, it was once hijacked by Chechen rebels in August 1999. It was able to resume operations following this.

Pictured on the runway at Guangzhou Airport in the south of China, in October 1999, is Tupolev Tu-154M B-2624 c/n 886 of Sichuan Airlines. The carrier, which still operates, is based at Cheng Du and now has an all-Airbus fleet. Across China, the use of the Tu-154 – and in fact all the Russian-built aircraft – was very much in the decline at the end of the 1990s. This aircraft was sold to a Russian airline and was later broken up.

On the move at Frankfurt Airport, in June 1997, is Tupolev TU-154M RA-85699 c/n 874 of Sibir Airlines. Note that the name on this aircraft is in the Russian Cyrillic lettering. Following their takeover of Vnukovo Airways in 2001, Sibir Airlines used a Moscow base to expand their route network into Europe and the Middle East. The Siberian carrier was based in Novosibirsk and following rebranding now operates today as S7 Airlines. This aircraft was withdrawn from use at base in 2009 and broken up in March 2015.

Pictured in August 1995 at its home base of Vnukovo International Airport, Moscow, is Tupolev Tu-154M RA-85618 c/n 737 of Vnukovo Airlines. This carrier once had one of the largest fleets of the type of aircraft. The carrier was bought by Sibir Airlines and is now part of S7 Airlines. This aircraft was withdrawn from service in 2008 and broken up in 2013.

Pictured in September 1997 at Mariscal Sucre International Airport, Quito, is Tupolev Tu-154M CU-T1265 c/n 751 of Cubana, the national airline of Cuba. This aircraft was sold on and operated with a number of Eastern European airlines before it was broken up.

The 1990s saw the European Airbus consortium grow and grow, eventually taking on Boeing in the United States. One of the types that broke all sales records was the single-aisle, narrow-body A320 family. The smallest, at that time, was the A319. It was shorter than the A320 by 5ft 3in (1.6m) forward and 7ft (2.13m) aft of the wing and it first flew in August 1995. Pictured at Zürich Airport, in August 1998, is Airbus A319-112 9A-CTG c/n 767 of Croatia Airlines. Based in Zagreb, they are the nation's flag carrier and this aircraft is still in service with them.

On the move at Frankfurt Airport, in June 1997, is Airbus A319-114 D-AILK c/n 679 of German national carrier Lufthansa. This aircraft is still in service with them. The configuration of the interior is 126 seats and the power plants are a pair of CFM-56-5A5 turbofan engines.

The A320 was the first of the single-aisle models to be launched, and first took to the air in February 1987. About to touch down in October 1999 at Guangzhou Airport, China, is Airbus A320-214 B-2362 c/n 828 of Shanghai-based China Eastern Airline. This carrier continues to be one of the largest of the current airlines in the nation. This aircraft was sold on, stored in Kemble, UK, and broken up for spare parts in 2019.

Arriving back to base at Guangzhou Airport, China, in October 1997, is Airbus A320-232 B-2352 c/n 720 of China Southern Airlines. The power plants for this aircraft are a pair of IAE V2527-5 turbofans; this type could have either these or CFM-56-5A5s depending upon the customer airline's choice. This aircraft is configured for eight business and 150 economy passengers and is still operating with the carrier.

Pictured at a wet Miami International Airport, in November 1992, is Airbus A320-212 N483GX c/n 189 of LASCA (Líneas Aéreas de Costa Rica). In 2004, they were taken over to become TACA Costa Rica. This aircraft was sold on and had multiple users until it was withdrawn from use in November 2015 in Chateauroux, France, and later broken up.

Landing at Manchester Airport, in August 1995, is Airbus A320-231 G-BVZU c/n 280 of Airworld. They were a holiday charter operator with bases at both Manchester Airport and Cardiff Airport. They were later merged into Flying Colours. This aircraft was sold on, had multiple users and withdrawn from use and stored in 2010.

Landing at their base of London Heathrow, in July 1995, is Airbus A320-231 G-MEDA c/n 480 of British Mediterranean Airways. In 2007, this carrier was taken over by British Midland International. This aircraft is currently operated by an airline in Iran.

Taxiing to its gate at Amsterdam Airport Schiphol, in August 1997, is Airbus A320-231 EI-TLG c/n 428 of Turkish Airlines, that nation's flag carrier. At the time of photographing, this aircraft is on lease, hence the Irish registration. This aircraft now operates for a carrier in Tajikistan.

About to land at Manchester Airport, in March 1993, is Airbus A320-212 G-HAGT c/n 294 of Excalibur Airways. They were a holiday charter operator with bases at Manchester Airport and London Gatwick. They suspended operations in June 1996. This aircraft was sold on and leased to many operators until it was withdrawn from service in October 2012. It was put into store in Marana, Arizona, and later broken up.

Seen in October 1999 at Guangzhou Airport, China, is Airbus A320-214 S7-ASG c/n 617 of Vietnam Airlines. This is a leased aircraft, as so many are now, and it is registered in the Seychelles; it does not carry the 'VN' prefix of Vietnam. This aircraft is currently serving with a company in Iran.

Coming in to land at London Gatwick, in August 1997, is Airbus A320-231 TC-ONG c/n 361 of Istanbul-based Onur Air. They are a Turkish holiday charter operator. Sold on, this aircraft is currently operated in Iran.

Landing at Athens International Airport, in June 1993, is Airbus A320-211 CS-TNE c/n 395 of TAP Air Portugal, the national airline. This aircraft was sold on and, like so many, is now operated by an Iranian airline.

Pictured at Manchester Airport, in March 1997, is Airbus A320-231 5B-DBB c/n 256 of Eurocypria Airlines. The holiday charter carrier, a subsidiary of Cyprus Airways, was based at Larnaca and suspended operations in November 2010. This aircraft is in operation with an airline in Bulgaria.

Against the clear blue sky above Athens International Airport, in June 1993, is Airbus A320-212 A40-EA c/n 313 of Gulf Air. The airline was, at that time, the multinational airline of the following states: Bahrain, Oman, Qatar, and Abu Dhabi. They are now the national airline of the Kingdom of Bahrain only as all of the other states have, over a number of years, formed their own national airlines. This aircraft was sold on and used by several airlines before being broken up in 2009.

The A321 is the longest of the single-aisle models. It increased the fuselage stretch found on the A320 by 14ft (4.26m) forward and 8ft 9in (2.66m) aft of the wing. It first flew in March 1993. Pictured at Shanghai, in October 1999, is Airbus A321-131 CS-MAB c/n 557 of Air Macau. At that time, Macau was still a colony of Portugal, hence the 'CS' prefix on the registration. Two months later, in December 1999, they became a semi-autonomous territory of mainland China and the registration prefix changed to 'B'. This aircraft became B-MAB; it was configured with 16 business and 162 economy seats. It served with Air Macau until it was put into store at Ireland West Airport Knock at the end of 2013 and later broken up.

The first of the Airbus designs, the A300, flew from Toulouse-Blagnac Airport, in October 1972, and paved the way for thousands of aircraft to follow. The A300 was a twin-aisle, twin-engine wide-body airliner that could seat, depending upon layout, up to 300+ passengers. Pictured at Manchester Airport, in June 1996, is Airbus A300B4-120 OY-CNL c/n 128 of Danish holiday charter carrier Premiair. In May 2002, they merged into My Travel Airways A/S and this aircraft went to a Turkish airline. It is now in store.

Breaking into a protected market is not easy, so Airbus had to think creatively. In 1977, they came up with the idea to lease four A300s to Eastern Air Lines, a major United States carrier, for six months, free of charge. This action knocked down the walls and the A300 and other Airbus designs have sold well in the United States ever since. Pictured at Manchester Airport, in May 1998, is Airbus A300B4-203 EI-TLK c/n 161 of Irish wet-lease company TransAer International Airlines. With bases at Dublin Airport, Manchester Airport and London Gatwick, they operated services for both scheduled and holiday charter companies around Europe and beyond. The company suspended operations in October 2000 and this 314 seat, all-economy aircraft was broken up in Filton, UK, in April 2003.

Pictured in March 1997 at Sharjah International Airport, UAE, is Airbus A300B4-203 VT-EHC c/n 181 of Indian Airlines. Delhi-based and government-owned, most of this airline's operations were domestic and regional international. In July 2007, they were merged into Air India. This aircraft was broken up in April 2009.

On approach to land at Manchester Airport, in March 1994, is Airbus A300B4-103 OO-MKO c/n 65 of European Airlines. Based in Brussels, the airline suspended operations at the start of 1996. This aircraft was sold on to a Turkish carrier and later broken up at Perpignan, France, in 2000.

The A300-600 series had a 21in (53.34cm) fuselage stretch and a new 'glass cockpit' fitted. It now had a flight deck crew of two; the post of flight engineer had been made redundant by the new instrument layout. Landing in October 1999 at Guangzhou Airport, China, is Airbus A300B4-622R B-2329 c/n 762 of China Northern Airlines. They were based in Shenyang Airport and flew domestic and regional international routes with a high-density configuration of 24 first and 250 economy seats. In November 2004, they were taken over by China Southern Airlines. This aircraft was sold on and now operates in Iran.

Seen in October 1999 at Xi'an Xianyang International Airport, China, is Airbus A300B4-622R JA8562 c/n 679 of JAS (Japan Air System). They were one of the largest operators of the A300 and had 35 in their fleet. The newer -600 series were powered by Pratt & Whitney PE4158 power plants, whilst the older A300s had General Electric CF-6 -50C2R engines. Based at Haneda Airport, Tokyo, JAS were taken over and rebranded as Japan Airlines Domestic in April 2004. This aircraft was converted to a freighter in 2012 and is currently in operation with a carrier in Germany.

Showing off its smart livery at Bangkok, in November 1999, is Airbus A300B4-622R B-18571 c/n 529 of China Airlines of Taipei. The airline flew this aircraft type around both southeast and northeast Asia, having operated the A300 since August 1982, when they launched a service to Manila, Philippines. This aircraft was sold on, had multiple users and is currently in store.

Emirates, the flag carrier of Dubai, have grown to be one of the largest carriers in the world with regard to their route network. The first A300s in their service were leased from other carriers, starting in November 1985. With these leased aircraft, they operated services around the Middle East and the Indian subcontinent. Although they no longer operate this type, Emirates first new purpose-built -600 series arrived in May 1989. Pictured on approach to Manchester Airport, in March 1994, is Airbus A300B4-605R A6-EKM c/n 701. The layout for the aircraft was 18 first, 42 business and 163 economy seats. It was sold on and now operates for a carrier in Iran.

Pictured in November 1992 on the runway at Luis Muñoz Marín International Airport, San Juan, is Airbus A300B4-605R N70072 c/n 515 of American Airlines. The giant United States carrier was the launch customer for the extended range variant and placed an order for 25, with ten more as options – these additional purchases took their total Airbus fleet to 35. It entered service with them in May 1988. It was mainly used around the Caribbean region and flew the carrier's hubs at Miami International Airport and New York JFK and LaGuardia; it also operated across the Atlantic. This aircraft was put into store in Roswell, New Mexico, in May 2009 and was later broken up.

On its way to depart from Sharjah International Airport, UAE, in March 1997, is Airbus A300B4-622 F-ODTK c/n 252 of Khartoum-based Sudan Airways, the national flag carrier. Services are flown to London, Paris and a number of locations within Africa. The configuration of this Pratt & Whitney PW4158 powered aircraft is 26 first and 249 economy class seats. It is currently in store with Sudan Airways at their base.

The A310 was the second Airbus design to see service. The fuselage was shorter than the A300 by 22ft 8in (6.9m) and it had a smaller wing area. The first flight was from Toulouse-Blagnac Airport in April 1982. It had a much longer range than the A300, with the -300 variant being able to fly 5,000 miles (8047km). Airline customers had a choice of either the Pratt & Whitney JT9D-7R or General Electric CF-6-80 turbofan engines. About to touch down on runway 28 at Zürich Airport, in August 1998, is Airbus A310-325 HB-IPL c/n 640 of Balair/CTA, which was based at the airport. The company owned by Swissair flew holiday charters, they were renamed Belair in 2001. This aircraft was sold on to a number of carriers before being broken up in 2010.

Pictured in March 1997 at Sharjah International Airport, UAE, is Airbus A310-325 F-OHPS c/n 704 in the colours of Sana'a-based Yemenia – Yemen Airways. The aircraft has a French registration as it is on lease from Airbus. It has since been re-registered with the Yemeni prefix of '7O', and still serves the airline.

Uzbekistan Airways are the flag carrier for the former republic of the USSR, now an independent state in its own right. Pictured on approach to London Heathrow, in June 1996, is Airbus A310-324 F-OGQZ c/n 576 showing off its smart colour scheme. The Tashkent-based company flew to locations both East and West and their aircraft was configured with a three-class interior. The aircraft was withdrawn from service in 2012 and put into store pending a sale.

Pictured at Amsterdam Airport Schiphol, in October 1999, is Airbus A310-304 5Y-BEL c/n 416 of Kenya Airways. The national airline was the first in Africa to operate the A310. From their Nairobi base, they operated to European cities, the Middle East and the Indian subcontinent. This aircraft was sold on first to an airline in Jordan and was later withdrawn and stored in 2011. It was then broken up in Kemble, UK.

Armenia, once a former USSR republic, was now an independent country. In 1998, they chose the A310 to be the first addition of Western-built aircraft to their national fleet. Pictured at Frankfurt Airport, in June 1999, is Airbus A310-222 F-OGYW c/n 276 of Yerevan-based Armenian Airlines. They were formally the Aeroflot Armenian Directorate. Services were flown to several European cities from their base. Note the airline name on this side of the fuselage in the local script. The company was declared bankrupt in April 2004 and this aircraft was broken up.

Landing at London Heathrow, in June 1996, is Airbus A310-203 TC-JYK c/n 172 of Kibris Turkish Airlines (Cyprus Turkish Airlines). Based at Ercan, in Northern Cyprus, they were associated with Turkish Airlines. It is worth noting that Northern Cyprus is a state that only Turkey officially recognises. Operations were suspended in June 2010 and this aircraft is in store at Istanbul.

On approach to Manchester Airport in September 1996, is Airbus A310-324 C-GCIV c/n 451 of Air Club International. Based in Montreal, their role was to fly holiday charters to Europe and the Caribbean. They ceased operations in 1997. This aircraft, with a one-class 265 economy seat layout, was sold on to an operator in Spain. It was withdrawn from service in 2008 and broken up in 2009.

On the move at Beijing, in October 1999, is Airbus A310-222 B-2303 c/n 419 of China Northwest Airlines. They were based at Xi'an Xianyang International Airport, China, and were taken over and merged into China Eastern Airlines during 2003–04. This aircraft was sold to a company in Thailand but is currently in store.

Pictured in November 1992 at Jorge Wilstermann Airport, Cochabamba, Bolivia, is Airbus A310-304 CP-2232 c/n 562 of Lloyd Aéreo Boliviano. The company flew this aircraft on services around South America and as far north as Miami. It had a one-class, 245 all-economy seating configuration. They were the country's flag carrier but ceased operations in 2010. Whilst this aircraft had multiple users over the years, it is now in store.

Pictured in September 1995 at Sheremetyevo International Airport, Moscow, is Airbus A310-324 F-OGYN c/n 458 of Diamond Sakha Airlines. This airline was based at Chulman Neryungri Airport in the autonomous Republic of Sakha/Yakutia in the far north-east of Russia. The company merged with Sakha Avia National Aircompany in 1997. This aircraft was sold on and, in 2005, it was converted to a freighter at Dresden Airport, Germany, and operated by a US parcel service company until May 2014. Following this, it was put into store in Victorville, California.

Pictured at Manchester Airport, in May 1990, is Airbus A310-204 5B-DAX c/n 486 of Nicosia-based Cyprus Airways. This airline had chosen the A310 as a lower fuel-burn alternative to replace their Boeing 707s. This aircraft was their first to have the small winglets in place when delivered. The company suspended operations in January 2015. Since then, a new Russian-backed company started operations in 2017 using the original Cyprus Airways name. This A310 was sold on, stored in late 2010 and later broken up.

Airbus produced two new aircraft, both of which were derived from the A300; they were called the A330 and A340. The fuselage had the same cross-section as the A300 and both new types had the same basic fuselage and wing design. The most differentiating factor was the cockpit layout which was now fitted with an electronic flight instrument system (EFIS), fly-by-wire and new side stick controls. The A330 was a twin-engine designed for medium-haul routes and the A340 was powered by four engines for long-haul services. Pictured at Beijing, in October 1999, is Airbus A330-342 B-HYE c/n 177 of Dragonair. Based in Hong Kong, they were renamed Cathay Dragon in 2016 and then, in late 2020, were merged into their parent company, Cathay Pacific Airways. This aircraft was sold on to a company in Canada and, in February 2021, was in store in Marana, Arizona.

The A330 first flew in November 1992. Airline customers could choose between the Rolls-Royce Trent, the Pratt & Whitney P4000 or the General Electric CF-6-80E1 turbofan engines. Pictured at Manchester Airport, in June 1998, is Airbus A330-201 C-GGWB c/n 211 of Canada 3000. The carrier was a holiday charter operator based in Toronto. This aircraft was brand new, having only being delivered that month. It was designed in a one-class, all-economy 340 seating configuration and powered by General Electric engines. Following the downturn in world traffic after the September 2001 attacks on the United States, the company was declared bankrupt. This aircraft is currently with a company in Portugal.

Pictured at Beijing, in October 1999, is Airbus A330-223 OE-LAM c/n 223 of Austrian Airlines, the nation's flag carrier. It was powered by the Pratt & Whitney PW4168A engines and in a two-class layout with 30 business and 235 economy seats. The first of their fleet was delivered in August 1998. This aircraft was withdrawn from use in October 2017 and parted out for spares in Teruel, Spain.

The first A340 flew in October 1996 and was powered by four CFM-56-5C turbofans. Pictured about to land at Zürich Airport, in August 1998, is Airbus A340-211 OO-SCW c/n 014 of Sabena (Société Anonyme Belge d'Exploitation de la Navigation Aérienne). The Belgian national airline had a history dating back to 1923; sadly, especially for a carrier with such a long pedigree, Sabena closed in November 2001. This aircraft was in a two-class configuration with 54 business and 198 economy seats. It was sold to a company in Jordan in 2007, withdrawn from use in May 2014, stored, and broken up at Lourdes, France.

Heading for its gate at Terminal Two at Manchester Airport, in May 1998, is Airbus A340-313 B-HXC c/n 142 of Hong Kong-based Cathay Pacific Airways. The interior was in a three-class configuration. This aircraft stayed with the company until the start of 2016 when it was flown to Lourdes, France, for storage and to be broken up for parts.

On push back from its gate at Frankfurt Airport, in June 1997, is Airbus A340-211 F-OHPG c/n 074 of Philippine Airlines, the nation's current flag carrier. The French registration is owing to the aircraft being on lease from Airbus' finance company. The airline used the A340 on services from its base at Ninoy Aquino International Airport, Manila, to European cities in a three-class layout. This aircraft was sold on to a carrier in Argentina in June 1999 and it was withdrawn from use in 2014. It is in store in Victorville, California.

About to land on runway 28 at Zürich Airport, in August 1998, is Airbus A340-313 B-2387 c/n 201 of Air China. This airline got their first A340 in October 1997; their main operations were from their Beijing base to major European cities such as London, Rome, Paris, and Zürich. They also used this aircraft on busy domestic routes such as Beijing to Shanghai. Like most carriers, Air China opted for a three-class layout. This aircraft was withdrawn from use at the end of 2013, stored at Lourdes, France, and later broken up for parts.

Arriving at Frankfurt Airport, Germany, in June 1999, from its Indian Ocean island home is Airbus A340-312 3B-NAU c/n 076 of Air Mauritius, the nation's flag carrier. They received their first A340 in May 1994 and operated to Europe with them in a three-class configuration. This aircraft operated with the carrier until 2019, when it was withdrawn from use in St Athan, Wales, and broken up for parts.

Pictured on approach to London Heathrow, in July 1999, is Airbus A340-312 6Y-JMC c/n 048 of Air Jamaica. The bright colour scheme reflects the carrier's Caribbean origins. This was their first year of operating this type of aircraft. Like most of its kind, it was in a three-class layout. Sold on, it first operated in Canada and then Argentina and was withdrawn from use at the end of 2013. It was put into store in Goodyear, Arizona.

On the move at Manchester Airport, in June 1996, is Airbus A340-300 G-VSUN c/n 114 of Virgin Atlantic Airways. The airline has always had a high profile because of its founder, Richard Branson. One of the regular routes was the popular holiday service from Manchester Airport to Orlando International Airport. This aircraft was withdrawn from use in 2015 and, after a short period of storage in France, went to Sanford, Florida, to be broken up.

Air Canada was the first operator of the A340 in North America. Before their own aircraft arrived, they leased some from International Lease Finance Corporation (ILFC) in 1995. One of these is pictured landing at London Heathrow, in July 1997; it is Airbus A340-313 C-FTNP c/n 093. The company did not operate a first class and so the configuration was 44 business and 220 economy seats. It was sold on first to an operator in the Caribbean and then to one in Argentina. It was withdrawn from use in April 2014 and stored in Goodyear, Arizona, with a view to part it out for spares.

The Concorde was perhaps the most famous airliner of all time; it was an example of aeronautical engineering at its peak. It flew passengers at speeds and heights that may never be equalled. Pictured at Zürich Airport, in August 1998, is BAe/Aérospatiale Concorde 101 F-BVFB c/n 207 of Air France, one of the two carriers to purchase the aircraft. The power plants were four Rolls-Royce Olympus 593-610 jets and the layout was 100 one-class seats. Following a fatal crash of one of their fleet, in July 2000, Air France took the aircraft out of service. This aircraft is preserved at the Auto and Technik Museum at Sinsheim, Germany.